# Adapted Reading and Study Workbook

Science Explorer

PRENTICE HALL **Physical Science**

PEARSON

Prentice Hall

Boston, Massachusetts
Upper Saddle River, New Jersey

ISBN 0-13-166598-7
7 8 9 10 11 12 13    12 11 10 09

# Physical Science

3

Introduction to Physical Science

# What Is Physical Science? (pages 6–9)

## How Scientists Think (pages 7–8)

*Key Concept:* Scientists use the skills of observing, inferring, and predicting to learn more about the natural world.

• **Science** is a way of learning about the natural world by gathering information.

• **Observing** means using your senses to gather information. You can make either quantitative observations or qualitative observations.

• **Quantitative observations** deal with numbers—the amount of something.

• **Qualitative observations** deal with descriptions that do not include numbers.

• **Inferring** is explaining or interpreting the things you observe. When you infer, you make an inference.

• **Predicting** means making a forecast of what will happen in the future. You make a prediction based either on what you have experienced in the past or on current evidence.

*Answer the following questions. Use your textbook and the ideas above.*

1. Circle the letter of each item that you would base a prediction on.
   a. evidence that you have recently collected
   b. a feeling about what will happen
   c. your experience in the past

**Introduction to Physical Science**

2. Draw a line from each term to its meaning.

| Term | Meaning |
|------|---------|
| science | **a.** observations that deal with numbers |
| observing | **b.** explaining or interpreting the things you observe |
| quantitative observations | **c.** using your senses to gather information |
| qualitative observations | **d.** a way of learning about the natural world |
| inferring | **e.** making a forecast of what will happen in the future |
| predicting | **f.** observations that deal with descriptions that do not include numbers |

3. The picture below shows a spider called a tarantula. Circle the letter of a quantitative observation about this animal.

   **a.** A tarantula is scary.

   **b.** A tarantula has eight legs.

   **c.** A tarantula eats insects.

Introduction to Physical Science

# The Study of Matter and Energy (pages 8–9)

***Key Concept:* Physical science is the study of matter, energy, and the changes they undergo.**

- Physical science is divided into two main areas: chemistry and physics.

- **Chemistry** is the study of the properties of matter. It also is the study of how matter changes.

- **Physics** is the study of matter and energy. It is also the study of how matter and energy interact. Topics in physics include motion, forces, forms of energy, sound, light, electricity, and magnetism.

*Answer the following questions. Use your textbook and the ideas above.*

4. Read each word in the box. In each sentence below, fill in one of the words.

| chemistry | biology | physics |

a. The study of matter and energy is called

_____.

b. The study of the properties of matter and how

matter changes is called _____.

5. Circle the letter of each topic that is included in physics.
   a. forms of energy
   b. sound
   c. how matter changes

**Introduction to Physical Science**

# Scientific Inquiry (pages 10–16)

## The Process of Inquiry (pages 10–14)

*Key Concept:* **The processes that scientists use in inquiry include posing questions, developing hypotheses, designing experiments, collecting and interpreting data, drawing conclusions, and communicating ideas and results.**

- **Scientific inquiry** refers to the different ways scientists study the natural world.

- Not all questions are scientific. Scientific questions are questions that you can answer by making observations. Scientific inquiry cannot answer questions based on opinions, values, or judgments.

- To answer a scientific question, a scientist develops a hypothesis. A **hypothesis** (plural: *hypotheses*) is a possible explanation or answer to a scientific question.

- Scientists can test a hypothesis by designing an experiment. They begin to plan their experiment by first looking at all the variables. A **variable** is a factor that can change in an experiment.

- In a scientific experiment, only one variable is changed on purpose. The variable that is changed on purpose is called the **manipulated variable**. By changing the manipulated variable, another factor may change in response. The factor that may change in response to the manipulated variable is called the **responding variable**.

- **Data** are facts, figures, and other evidence that a scientist gathers by observation. Data can be organized in a table called a data table.

Name _____ Date _____ Class _____

**Introduction to Physical Science**

*Answer the following questions. Use your textbook and the ideas on page 8.*

1. The different ways scientists study the natural world is called scientific _____ .

2. Circle the letter of each scientific question.
   a. Why doesn't my CD player work?
   b. What is the best song on this CD?
   c. How long will this CD play?

3. Draw a line from each term to its meaning.

| Term | Meaning |
|------|---------|
| hypothesis | a. a factor that can change in an experiment |
| variable | b. facts, figures, and other evidence that a scientist gathers by observation |
| data | c. a possible explanation or answer to a scientific question |

4. Read each word in the box. In each sentence below, fill in correct word.

| manipulated | experimental | responding |
|-------------|--------------|------------|

   a. The variable that is changed on purpose in an experiment is called the _____ variable.
   b. The factor that may change in response to the manipulated variable is called the _____ variable.

**Introduction to Physical Science**

**5.** Is the following sentence true or false? A testable hypothesis is one that can be proved or disproved by experiment or observation. _____

**6.** The diagram below is a model of the scientific inquiry process. Circle the step in the process where a scientist can test a hypothesis.

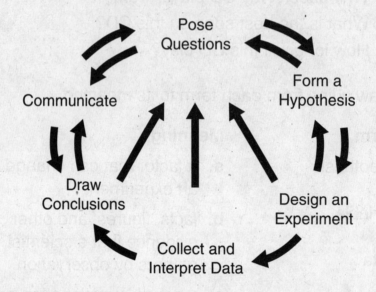

# How Science Develops (pages 15–16)

*Key Concept:* **Scientists use models and develop laws and theories to increase people's understanding of the natural world.**

• When a scientist cannot observe an object or a process, the scientist may make a model. A model might be a picture, a diagram, a computer image, or even a mathematical equation. A model represents—stands for—a real object or process.

• Certain models may look like the real thing. An example is a drawing of the solar system. Other models, such as a mathematical equation, are not meant to look like the real thing.

**Introduction to Physical Science**

- A **scientific law** is a statement that describes what scientists expect to happen every time certain conditions exist. For example, according to the law of gravity, when you drop a pencil, it will fall to the floor.

- A **scientific theory** is an explanation for a wide range of observations or experimental results. For example, the atomic theory says that all substances are made up of tiny particles called atoms.

- Scientists accept a scientific theory only when there is a lot of evidence that supports the theory.

*Answer the following questions. Use your textbook and the ideas on page 10 and above.*

**7.** Is the following sentence true or false? A model always looks like a real object. _____

**8.** Read each word in the box. In each sentence below, fill in one of the words.

| | | |
|---|---|---|
| law | hypothesis | theory |

**a.** An explanation for a wide range of observations or experimental results is a scientific

_____.

**b.** A statement that describes what scientists expect will happen every time certain conditions exist is a

scientific _____.

**Introduction to Physical Science**

# Science Laboratory Safety
## (pages 17–20)

## Safety in the Lab (pages 18–20)

*Key Concept:* **Good preparation helps you stay safe when doing science activities in the laboratory.**

- To prepare for work in a science laboratory, you must know how to use the equipment. Lab equipment might include a thermometer, balance, or graduated cylinder.

- You should begin preparing the day before the lab. Make sure you understand all the directions. Read the safety guidelines for any equipment you will be using.

- When performing a lab, the most important safety rule is: Always follow your teacher's instructions and the textbook directions exactly.

- Make sure you are familiar with all the safety symbols.

*Answer the following questions. Use your textbook and the ideas above.*

1. Circle the letter of when you should start preparing for a lab.
   a. the day before the lab
   b. an hour before the lab
   c. when the lab begins

2. Each of the pictures below is a laboratory safety symbol. Circle the letter of the safety symbol that warns you not to touch broken glassware.

a.          b.          c.

**Introduction to Physical Science**

## In Case of an Accident (page 20)

*Key Concept:* **When any accident occurs, no matter how minor, notify your teacher immediately. Then, listen to your teacher's directions and carry them out quickly.**

- Tell your teacher right away if there is an accident.

- Make sure you know where emergency equipment is in your lab room. Learn how to use the emergency equipment.

- Know what to do in if you cut yourself, burn yourself, spill something on your skin, or put something in your eye. For example, if you spill something on your skin, you and your teacher should pour large amounts of water on your skin.

*Answer the following questions. Use your textbook and the ideas above.*

3. Circle the letter of what you should do immediately if an accident occurs in the laboratory.

   a. Find emergency equipment.

   b. Ask another student what to do.

   c. Tell your teacher.

4. Is the following sentence true or false? Only the teacher needs to know where emergency equipment is in the laboratory. _____

**Introduction to Physical Science**

# What Is Technology? (pages 22–27)

## Introduction (page 22)

*Key Concept:* **Technology is closely related to science, but the two activities have different goals.**

- **Technology** is how people change the world around them. People create technology to meet their needs and to solve problems.

- The purposes of science and technology are very different. Science is the study of the natural world. In contrast, technology changes the natural world in order to solve problems.

- An **engineer** is a person who is trained to use both science and technology to solve problems.

*Answer the following questions. Use your textbook and the ideas above.*

1. Read each word in the box. In each sentence below, fill in one of the words.

   | science | engineer | technology |
   |---------|----------|------------|

   a. People create _____ to meet their needs and to solve problems.

   b. A person who is trained to use both science and technology to solve problems is a(an)

      _____.

2. Is the following sentence true or false? The goal of technology is the same as the goal of science.

   _____

Introduction to Physical Science

# Technology Design Process (pages 23–25)

*Key Concept:* **Often, engineers follow a common process: They identify a need, research the problem, design a solution, build and evaluate a prototype, troubleshoot and redesign, and communicate the solution.**

- An important activity in designing a solution to a problem is brainstorming. **Brainstorming** is when group members talk about any solutions that come to mind.

- To answer questions about whether a design will work, engineers must think about the constraints of a design. A **constraint** is anything that limits a design or causes a problem in the design.

- An engineering team may make trade-offs. A **trade-off** is when one good design feature is dropped in order to include another good design feature.

- A **prototype** is a working model used to test a design. Some prototypes are full-sized models. They work just as the final product will work. Today, many prototypes are "virtual" prototypes on a computer.

- **Troubleshooting** is studying a problem with the design and then fixing the problem.

*Answer the following questions. Use your textbook and the ideas above.*

3. Circle the letter of each sentence that is true about the technology design process.
   a. The process begins with identifying a need.
   b. Engineers never redesign a technology.
   c. Today, many prototypes are "virtual" on a computer.

**Introduction to Physical Science**

**4.** Draw a line from each term to its meaning.

| Term | Meaning |
|------|---------|
| brainstorming | **a.** studying a problem with the design and then fixing the problem |
| constraint | |
| trade-off | **b.** a working model used to test a design |
| prototype | **c.** when group members talk about any solutions that come to mind |
| troubleshooting | **d.** anything that limits or restricts a design |
| | **e.** when one good design feature is dropped in order to include another good design feature |

# Technology as a System (page 26)

*Key Concept:* **A technological system includes a goal, inputs, processes, outputs, and, in some cases, feedback.**

- A **system** is a group of parts that work together. You can think of a technology product as a system. A gas oven is an example of a technology product.

- A goal of a system is the purpose of the system.

- An input of a system is something that is put into the system in order to reach the goal. A process of a system is the series of actions that happens in the system. An output of a system is a result or a product.

- Some technological systems have feedback. Feedback is information a system uses to make sure the system meets the goal.

**Introduction to Physical Science**

*Answer the following questions. Use your textbook and the ideas on page 16.*

**5.** Complete the table about technology as a system.

| Technology as a System | |
|---|---|
| **Term** | **Meaning** |
| a. _____ | a group of parts that work together |
| Goal | the purpose of the system |
| b. _____ | something that is put into the system in order to reach the goal |
| Process | the series of actions that happens in the system |
| c. _____ | a result or a product of the system |
| d. _____ | information a system uses to make sure the system meets the goal |

**6.** Is the following sentence true or false? A gas oven is a technological system. _____

**Introduction to Physical Science**

# Technology and Society (page 27)

*Key Concept:* **Throughout history, from the Stone Age to the Information Age today, technology has had a large impact on society.**

- A society is a group of people who live together in an area and have things in common. For example, Americans form a society.

- During the Stone Age, people used stones to make tools. They made spears, axes, and shovels.

- You live in the Information Age. Today's technology includes cellular phones, satellites, and computers.

*Answer the following questions. Use your textbook and the ideas above.*

7. A group of people who live together in an area and have things in common is a(an)

   _____.

8. Is the following sentence true or false? In every age of history, technology has had a large impact on society.

   _____

# Describing Matter (pages 34–43)

## Properties of Matter (pages 35–37)

*Key Concept:* **Every form of matter has two kinds of properties—physical properties and chemical properties.**

- **Matter** is anything that has mass and takes up space. All the "stuff" around you is matter. Your pencil is matter. Water is matter. Air is matter, too.

- A **physical property** is how matter looks, feels, smells, sounds, and tastes. One physical property of water is that it is a liquid at room temperature. Other physical properties are color, hardness, and being able to stick to magnets.

- A **chemical property** tells how matter can change into new kinds of matter. For example, being able to catch fire and burn is a chemical property of wood. Another chemical property is being able to rust.

*Answer the following questions. Use your textbook and the ideas above.*

1. Anything that has mass and takes up space is
   a. matter.
   b. a physical property.
   c. a chemical property.

**Introduction to Matter**

**2.** Complete the table below. Decide if each property of matter is a physical property or a chemical property. Write *P* if it is a physical property. Write *C* if it is a chemical property.

| Properties of Matter | |
|---|---|
| **Property** | **Physical Property or Chemical Property?** |
| Rusting | **a.** |
| Color | **b.** |
| Burning | **c.** |
| Hardness | **d.** |

# Elements (pages 38–39)

***Key Concept:*** **Elements are the simplest substances.**

- An **element** is a kind of matter that cannot be broken down into any other kind of substance. Gold is an element. Iron and oxygen are elements, too.

- Every element has different physical properties. Every element also has different chemical properties.

- An **atom** is the smallest part of an element. Each element is made up of only one kind of atom. The atoms of gold are different from the atoms of iron.

- Most atoms can join with other atoms. Joining forms a **chemical bond**, which is a pulling force that holds atoms together.

**Introduction to Matter**

*Answer the following questions. Use your textbook and the ideas on page 20.*

3. Read each word in the box. In each sentence below, fill in one of the words.

| molecule | element | atom |
|---|---|---|

   a. The smallest part of an element is a(an)

   _____.

   b. A substance that cannot be broken down into any other kind of substance is called a(an)

   _____.

4. A pulling force that holds atoms together is called a

   a. substance.

   b. chemical bond.

   c. chemical property.

# Compounds (page 40)

*Key Concept:* **When elements are chemically combined, they form compounds having properties that are different from those of the uncombined elements.**

- **Compounds** are made up of the atoms of two or more elements joined together. The joined atoms are held together by chemical bonds.

- When elements combine, their physical properties and chemical properties change. A compound has properties different from each element it is made of.

**Introduction to Matter**

*Answer the following questions. Use your textbook and the ideas on page 21.*

5. The picture shows a model of a carbon atom and an oxygen atom. The picture also shows a compound formed when an atom of carbon joins with an atom of oxygen. Circle the letter of the compound.

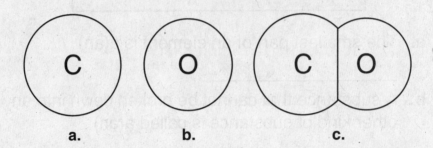

a.  b.  c.

6. Circle the letter of each sentence that is true about elements in compounds.

   a. When elements combine, their properties stay the same.

   b. When elements combine, their properties change.

   c. When elements combine, they have no properties.

## Mixtures (pages 41–43)

*Key Concept:* **Each substance in a mixture keeps its individual properties. Also, the parts of a mixture are not combined in a set ratio.**

- A **mixture** is made up of two or more compounds or elements that are together in the same place.

- A mixture is different from a compound in two ways:
   1. The parts of a mixture are not chemically combined.
   2. The properties of each part of a mixture do not change when the parts are mixed together. For example, when you mix sugar into water, you can still taste the sugar.

**Introduction to Matter**

- A **solution** is one kind of mixture. In a solution, the parts are very evenly mixed together. A mixture of sugar and water is a solution.

- In other mixtures, you can see the different parts. For example, you can see the lettuce, tomatoes, and olives in a salad.

- A mixture is easy to separate into its different parts because the parts keep their properties. For example, you can pick the olives out of a salad.

*Answer the following questions. Use your textbook and the ideas on page 22 and above.*

7. Read each word in the box. In each sentence below, fill in one of the words.

| mixture   molecule   solution |
| --- |

    **a.** A kind of mixture in which the different parts are very evenly mixed is called a

    _____.

    **b.** Two or more compounds or elements together in the same place is called a

    _____.

8. Is the following sentence true or false? Each part of a mixture keeps its properties. _____

**Introduction to Matter**

# Measuring Matter (pages 44–48)

## Weight and Mass (pages 44–45)

*Key Concept:* **Unlike weight, mass does not change with location, even when the force of gravity on an object changes.**

- **Weight** measures the pull of gravity on an object. Weight changes in different places. You would weigh less on the moon than on Earth.

- **Mass** is the amount of matter in an object. The amount of matter in an object does not change in different places. Your body would have the same mass on both the moon and Earth.

- Mass is measured in grams or kilograms.

*Answer the following question. Use your textbook and the ideas above.*

1. Read each word in the box. In each sentence below, fill in one of the words.

| weight | mass | grams |
|--------|------|-------|

   **a.** The amount of matter in an object is the object's
   _____.

   **b.** The measure of the pull of gravity on an object is
   the object's _____.

Introduction to Matter

## Volume (page 46)

***Key Concept:*** **Common units of volume include the liter (L), milliliter (mL), and cubic centimeter ($cm^3$).**

- **Volume** is how much space matter takes up.

- The volume of a liquid is measured in liters and milliliters. The volume of a solid is measured in cubic centimeters. One cubic centimeter is equal to one milliliter.

- You can find the volume of some solids by measuring their length, width, and height. Then you multiply these measurements.

Volume = Length x Width x Height

*Answer the following questions. Use your textbook and the ideas above.*

2. Which units are used to measure volume?
   a. grams
   b. cubic centimeters
   c. mass

3. The picture shows the length, width, and height of a block of wood. Use these measurements to find the volume of the block of wood. The volume is

   _____.

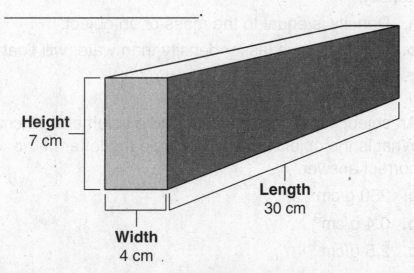

**Height**
7 cm

**Length**
30 cm

**Width**
4 cm

**Introduction to Matter**

## Density (pages 47–48)

*Key Concept:* **You can determine the density of a sample of matter by dividing its mass by its volume.**

- **Density** relates the mass of an object to its volume. Density can be described as grams per cubic centimeter or $g/cm^3$.

- You can find the density of an object by measuring the object's mass and volume. Then you divide the mass of the object by its volume.

$$\text{Density} = \frac{\text{Mass}}{\text{Volume}}$$

- Objects that have a lot of mass in a small volume are very dense. Objects with a small amount of mass in a large volume are less dense.

- Water has a density of 1 $g/cm^3$. Objects with a greater density than water will sink. Objects with a lesser density than water will float.

- Density is a physical property of matter.

*Answer the following questions. Use your textbook and the ideas above.*

4. Circle the letter of each sentence that is true about density.
   a. Density is equal to the mass of an object.
   b. Objects with a lesser density than water will float.
   c. Density is a physical property.

5. An object has a mass of 25 g and a volume of 10 $cm^3$. What is the object's density? Circle the letter of the correct answer.
   a. 250 $g/cm^3$
   b. 0.4 $g/cm^3$
   c. 2.5 $g/cm^3$

# Changes in Matter (pages 50–55)

## Physical Change (page 51)

***Key Concept:*** **A substance that undergoes a physical change is still the same substance after the change.**

- A **physical change** changes the way matter looks. It does not change the matter into a new kind of matter.

- Melting ice to form liquid water is a physical change. Dissolving sugar in water is another physical change. Bending a paperclip is also a physical change.

*Answer the following questions. Use your textbook and the ideas above.*

1. Is the following sentence true or false? A physical change changes matter into a new kind of matter.

   _____

2. Use the words in the box to complete the concept map about physical change.

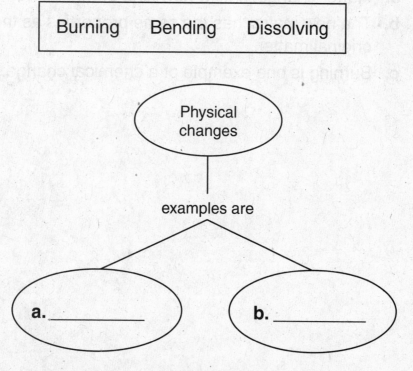

Burning    Bending    Dissolving

Physical changes

examples are

a. _____

b. _____

**Introduction to Matter**

## Chemical Change (pages 52–53)

***Key Concept:*** **Unlike a physical change, a chemical change produces new substances with properties different from those of the original substances.**

- In a **chemical change**, matter changes into a new kind of matter. The new matter has different properties from the original matter.

- Burning is one example of a chemical change. When wood burns, elements in the wood combine with oxygen in the air to form new matter. The new matter is ash and gases.

- Tarnishing is another kind of chemical change. Silver metal tarnishes when it combines with sulfur in the air and forms a dark coating on the metal.

*Answer the following question. Use your textbook and the ideas above.*

3. Circle the letter of each sentence that is true about chemical changes.

   a. Matter changes into a new kind of matter.

   b. The new matter has the same properties as the original matter.

   c. Burning is one example of a chemical change.

# Matter and Thermal Energy (pages 54–55)

*Key Concept:* **Every chemical or physical change in matter includes a change in energy.**

- **Energy** is the ability to do work. Energy can cause matter to change.

- When matter changes, energy can be given off. Burning wood gives off energy. Some changes take energy. Melting ice takes energy.

- **Thermal energy** is a kind of energy that is often given off or taken in when matter changes. You feel thermal energy as heat. Thermal energy always flows from warmer objects to cooler objects.

- **Temperature** tells the amount of thermal energy an object has. An object with a lot of thermal energy has a high temperature. An object with little thermal energy has a low temperature.

*Answer the following questions. Use your textbook and the ideas above.*

4. The ability to do work is called
   a. chemical change.
   b. energy.
   c. density.

5. Is the following sentence true or false? Thermal energy flows from warmer objects to cooler objects.

   _____

**Introduction to Matter**

6. Read each word in the box. In each sentence below, fill in one of the words.

| energy | high | low |
|--------|------|-----|

a. An object with a lot of thermal energy has a

_____ temperature.

b. An object with little thermal energy has a

_____ temperature.

# Energy and Matter (pages 58–61)

## Forms of Energy (pages 58–60)

*Key Concept:* **Forms of energy related to changes in matter may include kinetic, potential, chemical, electromagnetic, electrical, and thermal energy.**

- **Kinetic energy** is the kind of energy that a moving object has. **Potential energy** is the kind of energy that is stored in an object. Your bike at the top of a hill has only potential energy. When the bike is rolling down the hill, it has kinetic energy.

- **Chemical energy** is a kind of potential energy. Chemical energy is stored in chemical bonds between atoms. When the chemical bonds break and new bonds form, the potential energy changes into another form of energy, such as thermal energy.

- **Electromagnetic energy** is energy that travels in waves through the air. Light and radio waves are electromagnetic energy. **Electrical energy** is the energy of moving charged particles. Electrical energy causes a light bulb to light.

*Answer the following questions. Use your textbook and the ideas above.*

1. The picture shows a roller coaster. Draw an X to show where a roller coaster car would have the most potential energy.

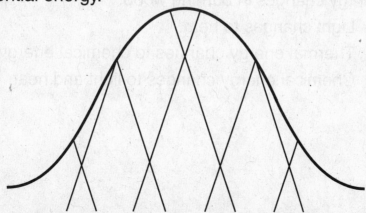

**Introduction to Matter**

**2.** Draw a line from each term to its meaning.

| Term | Meaning |
|---|---|
| chemical energy | **a.** energy that travels in waves through the air |
| electromagnetic energy | **b.** energy stored in chemical bonds between atoms |
| electrical energy | **c.** energy of moving charged particles |

## Transforming Energy (page 61)

*Key Concept:* **During a chemical change, chemical energy may be changed to other forms of energy. Other forms of energy may also be changed to chemical energy.**

- Chemical energy is stored in the chemical bonds of the elements that make up wood. When wood burns, this chemical energy changes to different kinds of energy. This chemical energy changes to light and heat. Light is electromagnetic energy. Heat is thermal energy.

- Plants change energy from the sun into chemical energy. Plants store the chemical energy as sugar.

*Answer the following questions. Use your textbook and the ideas above.*

**3.** Circle the letter of each sentence that is true about the energy changes in burning wood.

   **a.** Light changes to heat.

   **b.** Thermal energy changes to chemical energy.

   **c.** Chemical energy changes to light and heat.

**Introduction to Matter**

4. Plants change the energy from the sun into
   a. electrical energy.
   b. chemical energy.
   c. electromagnetic energy.

# States of Matter (pages 70–75)

## Solids (pages 71–72)

*Key Concept:* **The fixed, closely packed arrangement of particles causes a solid to have a definite shape and volume.**

- A **solid** is a kind of matter that has a fixed shape and a fixed volume. Your pencil is a solid. The shape and volume of your pencil will not change if you move the pencil from place to place.

- The different elements and compounds that make up matter are made of particles. The particles of a solid are packed closely together.

- The particles of a solid cannot move from their spot within the solid. However, the particles can move slightly back and forth in place.

*Answer the following questions. Use your textbook and the ideas above.*

1. Is the following sentence true or false? The particles that make up a solid do not move at all. _____

2. The picture shows two containers with particles of a kind of matter in each. Circle the letter of the container that shows how the particles of a solid are arranged.

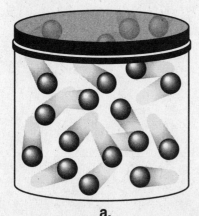

a.

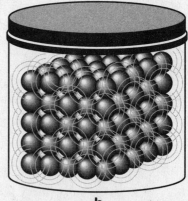

b.

**Solids, Liquids, and Gases**

## Liquids (pages 73–74)

***Key Concept:* Because its particles are free to move, a liquid has no definite shape. However, a liquid does have a definite volume.**

- A **liquid** is a kind of matter that has a fixed volume. However, the shape of a liquid changes with the shape of its container.

- Water is a liquid. As you pour water from one cup to another, the shape of the water changes to match the shape of the cup. The volume of the water stays the same.

- The particles of a liquid are packed closely together. However, these particles can move away from their spots.

*Answer the following questions. Use your textbook and the ideas above.*

3. Which is a liquid?

   a. your desk

   b. a pencil

   c. milk

4. Read each word in the box. In each sentence below, fill in one of the words.

   | volume | shape | particles |
   | --- | --- | --- |

   a. A liquid changes _____ depending on the liquid's container.

   b. A liquid has a definite _____ no matter what container the liquid is in.

Solids, Liquids, and Gases

## Gases (page 75)

**Key Concept: As they move, gas particles spread apart, filling all the space available. Thus, a gas has neither definite shape nor definite volume.**

- A **gas** is a kind of matter that easily changes volume and shape.

- Air is a gas. When you blow air into a balloon, the air takes the shape of the balloon. When you let the air out of the balloon, the particles spread out into the room.

- Gas particles can move around freely. Gas particles can either spread apart or be squeezed together.

*Answer the following questions. Use your textbook and the ideas above.*

5. Which is a gas?
    a. fruit juice
    b. air
    c. books

6. Is the following sentence true or false? Gas particles can move around freely. _____

**Solids, Liquids, and Gases**

# Changes of State (pages 76–81)

## Changes Between Solid and Liquid (pages 77–78)

*Key Concept:* **At its melting point, the particles of a solid substance are vibrating so fast that they break free from their fixed positions. At its freezing temperature, the particles of a liquid are moving so slowly that they begin to form regular patterns.**

• When a solid changes to a liquid, the solid is **melting**. Solid ice melts in warm temperatures and forms liquid water.

• When a solid gains thermal energy, the particles of the solid move in place faster. When enough energy is added, the particles break away from their places.

• When a liquid changes to a solid, the liquid is **freezing**. Freezing is just the reverse of melting. Liquid water freezes in very cold temperatures and forms ice.

• When a liquid loses thermal energy, the particles of the liquid slow down. Over time, the particles move into fixed places. Then, the liquid becomes solid.

*Answer the following questions. Use your textbook and the ideas above.*

1. Read each word in the box. In each sentence below, fill in the correct word or words.

| melting    freezing    thermal energy |
|---|

   a. When a liquid changes to a solid, the liquid is

   _____.

   b. When a solid changes to a liquid, the solid is

   _____.

**Solids, Liquids, and Gases**

2. Fill in the words in the table below to show the relationship between energy and the movement of particles.

| Changes Between Solid and Liquid | | |
|---|---|---|
| **Change of State** | **Thermal Energy** | **Particles Move** |
| Melting | added or gained | b. _____ |
| Freezing | a. _____ | slower |

3. Is the following sentence true or false? When a liquid becomes a solid, it gains thermal energy. _____

## Changes Between Liquid and Gas (pages 78–80)

*Key Concept:* **Vaporization takes place when the particles in a liquid gain enough energy to form a gas. Condensation occurs when particles in a gas lose enough thermal energy to form a liquid.**

- The change from a liquid to a gas is called **vaporization** (vay puhr ih ZAY shun). At high temperatures, water changes to water vapor. When a puddle of water disappears on a hot, sunny day, the water has changed to water vapor.

- When a liquid gains thermal energy, the particles of the liquid move faster. When enough energy is added, the particles spread far apart. Then, the liquid becomes a gas.

**Solids, Liquids, and Gases**

- The change from a gas to a liquid is called **condensation** (kahn dehn SAY shun). When water vapor cools, it becomes liquid water. Dew on the grass in the morning is water vapor in the air that has cooled and become a liquid.

- When gas particles lose thermal energy, they slow down. As the particles slow down, the particles move closer together and form a liquid.

*Answer the following questions. Use your textbook and the ideas on page 38 and above.*

**4.** Look at the pictures below. One shows a puddle of water on a sunny day. The other shows drops of dew as they form on grass. Circle the letter of the picture in which vaporization is occurring.

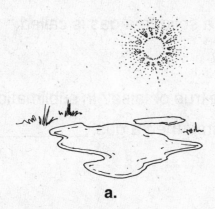

**a.**

**b.**

**5.** Read each word in the box. In each sentence below, fill in one of the words.

| | | |
|---|---|---|
| make | gain | lose |

**a.** Vaporization takes place when liquid particles

_____ thermal energy.

**b.** Condensation takes place when gas particles

**c.** _____ thermal energy.

**Solids, Liquids, and Gases**

# Changes Between Solid and Gas (page 81)

*Key Concept:* **During sublimation, particles of a solid do not pass through the liquid state as they form a gas.**

- The direct change from a solid to a gas is called **sublimation** (suhb luh MAY shun). In sublimation, the solid never changes to a liquid. When snow seems to disappear without melting, sublimation has taken place.

- Sublimation takes place when particles on the surface of a solid gain enough thermal energy to break away. The particles have enough energy to spread far apart and form a gas.

*Answer the following questions. Use your textbook and the ideas above.*

**6.** The direct change from a solid to a gas is called

_____.

**7.** Is the following sentence true or false? In sublimation, a solid becomes a liquid first, then a gas. _____

**Solids, Liquids, and Gases**

# Gas Behavior (pages 83–89)

## Measuring Gases (pages 84–85)

*Key Concept:* **When working with a gas, it is helpful to know its volume, temperature, and pressure.**

- Volume is the amount of space that matter takes up. The volume of a gas is the same as the volume of its container.

- Temperature tells the amount of thermal energy an object has. Temperature is a measure of the motion of the particles of matter. The faster the particles move, the higher the temperature. Gas particles move very fast.

- As gas particles move, they bump into the sides of their container. The **pressure** of a gas is the strength of its push on the walls of the container. Gas pressure is high when gas particles bump the sides of the container often and hard.

*Answer the following questions. Use your textbook and the ideas above.*

1. Draw a line from each term to its meaning.

| Term | Meaning |
|------|---------|
| pressure | **a.** the amount of space that matter takes up |
| temperature | **b.** a measure of the motion of particles of matter |
| volume | **c.** the strength of gas particles bumping into the sides of the container |

**Solids, Liquids, and Gases**

2. Circle the letter of each sentence that is true about gas behavior.
   a. The volume of a gas is the same as the volume of its container.
   b. The faster that gas particles move, the lower the temperature.
   c. Gas pressure is high when gas particles bump the sides of the container often and hard.

## Pressure and Volume (page 86)

*Key Concept:* **Robert Boyle found that when the pressure of a gas at constant temperature is increased, the volume of the gas decreases. When the pressure is decreased, the volume increases.**

- **Boyle's law** tells how the volume and the pressure of a gas are related when temperature stays the same.

- A gas with decreasing volume has increasing pressure.

- A gas with increasing volume has decreasing pressure.

*Answer the following questions. Use your textbook and the ideas above.*

3. According to Boyle's law, a gas with decreasing volume has
   a. increasing pressure.
   b. decreasing pressure.
   c. no pressure at all.

**Solids, Liquids, and Gases**

4. According to Boyle's law, a gas with increasing volume has
   a. increasing pressure.
   b. decreasing pressure.
   c. no pressure at all.

## Pressure and Temperature (page 87)

*Key Concept:* **When the temperature of a gas at constant volume is increased, the pressure of the gas increases. When the temperature is decreased, the pressure of the gas decreases.**

- At high temperatures, gas particles are moving fast. Fast-moving gas particles hit the walls of the container hard and often. The pressure of the gas is high.

- At low temperatures, gas particles are moving slowly. Slow-moving gas particles hit the walls of the container softly and less often. The pressure of the gas is low.

*Answer the following question. Use your textbook and the ideas above.*

5. Read each word in the box. In each sentence below, fill in one of the words.

| high | fast | low |
|------|------|-----|

a. At high temperature, gas particles have _____ pressure.

b. At low temperature, gas particles have _____ pressure.

**Solids, Liquids, and Gases**

# Volume and Temperature (pages 88–89)

*Key Concept:* **Jacques Charles found that when the temperature of a gas is increased at constant pressure, its volume increases. When the temperature of a gas is decreased at constant pressure, its volume decreases.**

- **Charles's law** tells how the temperature and the volume of a gas are related when gas pressure stays the same.

- At high temperatures, gas particles move fast and spread far apart. When gas particles move far apart, the gas takes up more space. The volume of the gas is large.

- At low temperatures, gas particles move slowly and close together. When gas particles move close together, the gas takes up less space. The volume of the gas is small.

*Answer the following question. Use your textbook and the ideas above.*

**6.** Look at the two balloons. Both balloons are filled with the same amount of gas.

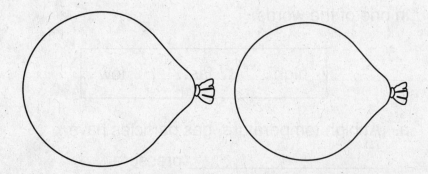

    **a.** Circle the balloon with the larger volume of gas.

    **b.** Underline the balloon at the higher temperature.

**Solids, Liquids, and Gases**

# Graphing Gas Behavior (pages 90–93)

## Temperature and Volume (pages 91–92)

*Key Concept:* **The graph of Charles's law shows that the volume of a gas is directly proportional to its kelvin temperature under constant pressure.**

- A **graph** shows how two things are related.

- The graph for Charles's law shows how temperature is related to volume. Temperature data are shown along the bottom line, or bottom axis, of the graph. Volume data are shown on the side axis of the graph.

- The dots along the line on the graph of Charles's law show the gas volume at different temperatures. For example, when the temperature of the gas was 303 kelvins, the volume of the gas was 56 mL.

- The line on the graph of Charles's law is straight and goes up from left to right. This line shows that as the temperature of a gas increases, its volume also increases.

*Answer the following questions. Use your textbook and the ideas above.*

1. The line for Charles's law shows that as the temperature of a gas increases, its volume

   **a.** stays the same.

   **b.** decreases.

   **c.** increases.

**Solids, Liquids, and Gases**

2. The graph shows Charles's law. Write *V* along the axis where volume measurements are shown. Write *T* along the axis where temperature measurements are shown.

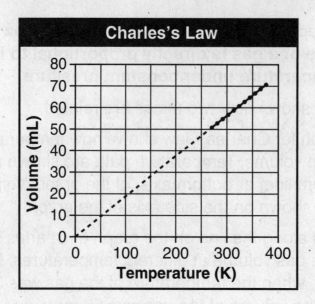

## Pressure and Volume (pages 92–93)

*Key Concept:* **The graph for Boyle's law shows that the pressure of a gas varies inversely with its volume at constant temperature.**

- The graph for Boyle's law shows how the volume and pressure of a gas are related. Volume data are shown along the bottom axis. Pressure data are shown on the side axis.

- The dots along the line on the graph of Boyle's law show the gas pressure at different volumes. For example, when the volume of the gas was 200 mL, the pressure of the gas was 30 kPa.

- The line on the graph of Boyle's law curves down from left to right. This line shows that as the volume of a gas increases, its pressure decreases.

Name _____ Date _____ Class _____

**Solids, Liquids, and Gases**

*Answer the following questions. Use your textbook and the ideas on page 46.*

3. The curved line in the graph for Boyle's law shows that as gas volume increases, gas pressure
   a. increases.
   b. decreases.
   c. stays the same.

4. The graph shows Boyle's law. Write *V* along the axis where volume measurements are shown. Write *P* along the axis where pressure measurements are shown.

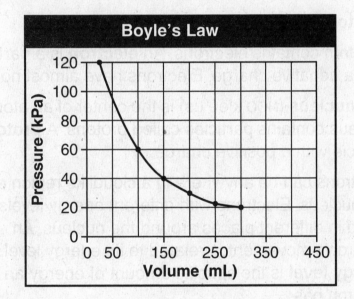

# Introduction to Atoms

(pages 102–108)

## Development of Atomic Models

(pages 103–105)

*Key Concept:* **Atomic theory grew as a series of models that developed from experimental evidence. As more evidence was collected, the theory and models were revised.**

- Different scientists suggested different models of the atom from the 1600s until today. Over time, models of the atom changed as scientists made new discoveries.

- An **atom** is the smallest piece of an element.

- An atom contains electrons. An **electron** is a particle with a negative charge. Electrons have almost no mass.

- The **nucleus** (NOO klee us) is the center of an atom. The nucleus contains particles called protons. A **proton** is a particle with a positive charge.

- Electrons can be anywhere in a cloudlike region around the nucleus. Electrons with different energy levels are found in different places around the nucleus. An electron's movement is related to its energy level. An **energy level** is the specific amount of energy an electron has.

*Answer the following questions. Use your textbook and the ideas above.*

1. The smallest piece of an element is a(an)

   _____.

2. Draw a line from each term to its meaning.

| Term | Meaning |
| --- | --- |
| electron | **a.** a particle of an atom with a positive charge |
| energy level | **b.** an area outside the nucleus where electrons with the same amount of energy are found |
| proton | **c.** a particle of an atom with a negative charge |

3. Is the following sentence true or false? Models of the atom changed over time as scientists made new discoveries. _____

4. The picture shows a model of an atom. Circle the nucleus of the atom.

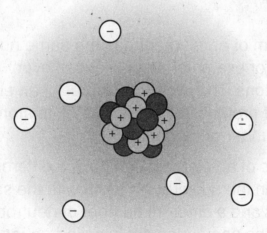

**Elements and the Periodic Table**

# The Modern Atomic Model (pages 106–108)

*Key Concept:* The modern atomic model describes an atom as consisting of a nucleus that contains protons and neutrons, surrounded by a cloudlike region of moving electrons.

- A **neutron** is a particle contained in the nucleus. A neutron is electrically neutral, which means that it has no charge.

- In an atom, the number of protons equals the number of electrons. As a result, the positive charge from the protons equals the negative charge from the electrons. The charges balance, making the atom neutral.

- A proton has almost 2,000 times the mass of an electron. A proton and a neutron are about equal in mass.

- Most of an atom's volume is the space in which the electrons move. Atoms themselves are extremely small. The tiniest speck of dust may contain 10 million billion atoms.

- Every atom of an element has the same number of protons. For example, the nucleus of every carbon atom has 6 protons. The **atomic number** of an element is the number of protons in the nucleus of its atoms. The atomic number of carbon is 6.

- The atoms of an element can have a different number of neutrons in the nucleus. An atom with the same number of protons and a different number of neutrons than other atoms of the same element is called an **isotope** (EYE suh tohp). An isotope is identified by its mass number. The **mass number** of an atom is the sum of the protons and neutrons in its nucleus.

Name _____ Date _____ Class _____

*Answer the following questions. Use your textbook and the ideas on page 50.*

5. Fill in the table below about the particles that make up an atom.

| Particles of an Atom | | |
|---|---|---|
| **Particles** | **Electric Charge** | **Location in an Atom** |
| Proton | positive | a. _____ |
| Electron | b. _____ | cloud around nucleus |
| c. _____ | no charge | nucleus |

6. Is the following sentence true or false? Every atom of an element has the same number of protons.

_____

7. Draw a line from each term to its meaning.

**Term**

atomic number

isotope

mass number

**Meaning**

a. an atom with the same number of protons and a different number of neutrons than other atoms of the same element

b. the sum of the protons and neutrons in an atom's nucleus

c. the number of protons in the nucleus of an atom of an element

# Organizing the Elements (pages 109–117)

## Patterns in the Elements (pages 110–113)

***Key Concept:*** **Dmitri Mendeleev noticed that a pattern of properties appeared when he arranged the elements in order of increasing atomic mass.**

- Mendeleev knew that some elements had similar physical and chemical properties. When Mendeleev arranged the elements in order of their atomic mass, the properties of the element fell into a pattern.

- The **atomic mass** of an element is the average mass of all the isotopes of that element. The mass number of an atom is equal to the number of protons and neutrons in the nucleus.

- The **periodic table** is a chart of the elements. The periodic table shows the repeating pattern of the chemical and physical properties of all the elements. In the current periodic table, the elements are arranged in order of atomic number.

*Answer the following questions. Use your textbook and the ideas above.*

1. Draw a line from each term to its meaning.

| Term | Meaning |
|---|---|
| atomic mass | **a.** a chart of the elements |
| periodic table | **b.** the average mass of all the isotopes of an element |

2. Is the following sentence true or false? The elements in the current periodic table are arranged in order of

   atomic mass. _____

**Elements and the Periodic Table**

# Organization of the Periodic Table (pages 114–115)

***Key Concept:*** **The properties of an element can be predicted from its location in the periodic table.**

- A row of elements in the periodic table is called a **period**. As you look at the elements in a period from the left side of the table to the right side, the properties of the elements change in the same way for every period.

- The elements on the left side of a period are metals that react with other elements very easily. Elements in the middle of the period do not react with other elements as easily. Elements at the right end of the table are nonmetals.

- A column of elements in the periodic table is called a **group**. Groups are also called families. The elements in each group have properties that are similar. For example, the elements in Group 1 are metals that react very quickly with water. The elements in Group 18 rarely react at all.

*Answer the following questions. Use your textbook and the ideas above.*

**3.** Read each word in the box. In each sentence below, fill in one of the words.

| element | period | group |
|---------|--------|-------|

**a.** A row of elements in the periodic table is called a(an) _____.

**b.** A column of elements in the periodic table is called a(an) _____.

**Elements and the Periodic Table**

4. Look at the outline of the periodic table below. Tell which is a group and which is a period.

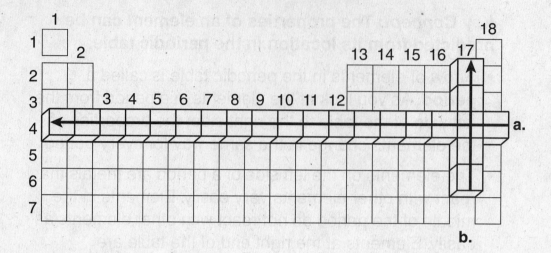

a. _____

b. _____

5. Circle the letter of each sentence that is true about the periodic table.

a. The elements in a period have properties that are the same.

b. The properties of the elements change in the same way for every period.

c. The elements in each group have properties that are similar.

6. Is the following sentence true or false? Groups are also called families. _____

**Elements and the Periodic Table**

**Key Concept:** Each square of the periodic table includes the element's atomic number, chemical symbol, name, and atomic mass.

- The periodic table has one square for each element. Each square has information about the element.

- In an element square, the top number is the atomic number of the element. For example, the atomic number for iron is 26. Iron has 26 protons. Iron also has 26 electrons.

- In the element square, the chemical symbol for the element is below the atomic number. A **chemical symbol** is one or two letters that stand for an element. The chemical symbol for iron is Fe.

- The bottom number in an element square is the atomic mass of the element. The atomic mass of iron is 55.847 amu (atomic mass units).

*Answer the following question. Use your textbook and the ideas above.*

7. The picture shows an element square from the periodic table. Look at the square to answer the questions.

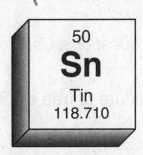

50
**Sn**
Tin
118.710

a. Write the name of the element. _____

b. Write the atomic number of the element.

_____

c. Write the chemical symbol of the element.

_____

**Elements and the Periodic Table**

# How Elements Form in Stars (pages 116–117)

*Key Concept:* Nuclear fusion, which occurs in stars on a huge scale, combines smaller nuclei into larger nuclei, creating heavier elements.

- The sun is made mostly of the element hydrogen.

- The sun is so hot that the matter making up the sun is not a solid, liquid, or gas. The matter making up the sun is plasma. **Plasma** is a mixture of free electrons and atomic nuclei without electrons.

- The pressure in stars is so high that the atomic nuclei are squeezed together. If these nuclei join, nuclear fusion takes place.

- In **nuclear fusion**, two atomic nuclei combine to form a larger nucleus of a new element. When nuclear fusion happens, huge amounts of energy are given off. The energy from the sun comes from nuclear fusion.

- Elements heavier than iron form when large stars explode in a supernova. A supernova is a huge explosion that breaks apart a very large star. The supernova gives off enough energy to form the heaviest elements.

*Answer the following questions. Use your textbook and the ideas above.*

**8.** Matter that is a mixture of free electrons and atomic nuclei is called

    **a.** a liquid.

    **b.** a solid.

    **c.** plasma.

**Elements and the Periodic Table**

**9.** The picture shows a nuclear fusion reaction. Draw a circle around the nucleus formed in the fusion reaction.

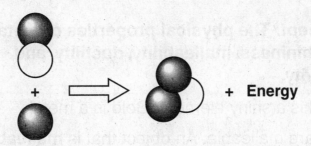

**10.** The heaviest elements are made from stars in an event called

    **a.** a supernova.

    **b.** isotope formation.

    **c.** plasma.

**Elements and the Periodic Table**

# Metals (pages 118–125)

## Properties of Metals (pages 118–119)

*Key Concept:* **The physical properties of metals include shininess, malleability, ductility, and conductivity.**

- A **metal** is a shiny element. Gold is a metal.

- Metals are malleable. An object that is **malleable** (MAL ee uh bul) can be hammered or rolled into a flat sheet. Malleability is a physical property.

- Metals are ductile. An object that is **ductile** can be pulled out into a long wire. Ductility is a physical property.

- Most metals are good conductors. **Conductivity** is the ability of an object to move heat or electricity to another object. Conductivity is a physical property.

- **Reactivity** is the ease and speed an atom has combining with other atoms. Reactivity is a chemical property. The atoms of some metals, like sodium, are very reactive. Atoms of gold are not very reactive.

- Metal atoms usually react with other atoms by losing electrons.

*Answer the following questions. Use your textbook and the ideas above.*

1. A metal is
   a. dull.
   b. a poor conductor.
   c. shiny.

2. Is the following sentence true or false? Reactivity is a chemical property. _____

**3.** Draw a line from each term to its meaning.

| Term | Meaning |
|------|---------|
| malleable | **a.** the ability to move heat or electricity to another object |
| ductile | **b.** able to be hammered or rolled into a flat sheet |
| conductivity | **c.** the ease and speed an atom has combining with other atoms |
| reactivity | **d.** able to be pulled out into a long wire |

## Metals in the Periodic Table (pages 120–124)

*Key Concept:* **The reactivity of metals tends to decrease as you move from left to right across the periodic table.**

- The metals in Group 1 of the periodic table are called **alkali metals**. Alkali metals are shiny and soft. These metals are the most reactive group of metals. In nature, these metals are always combined with other elements.

- The metals in Group 2 of the periodic table are called **alkaline earth metals**. Most alkaline earth metals are hard, gray-white, and good conductors. These metals are not as reactive as the metals in Group 1, but are more reactive than the other metals.

- The elements in Groups 3 through 12 are called the **transition metals**. Most transition metals are hard and shiny. All are good conductors. Some transition metals are gold, copper, and iron. These metals are less reactive than the metals in Groups 1 and 2.

- Only some of the elements in Groups 13 through 15 are metals. These metals are not very reactive.

**Elements and the Periodic Table**

*Answer the following questions. Use your textbook and the ideas on page 59.*

4. Read each word in the box. In the concept map below, fill in one of the words.

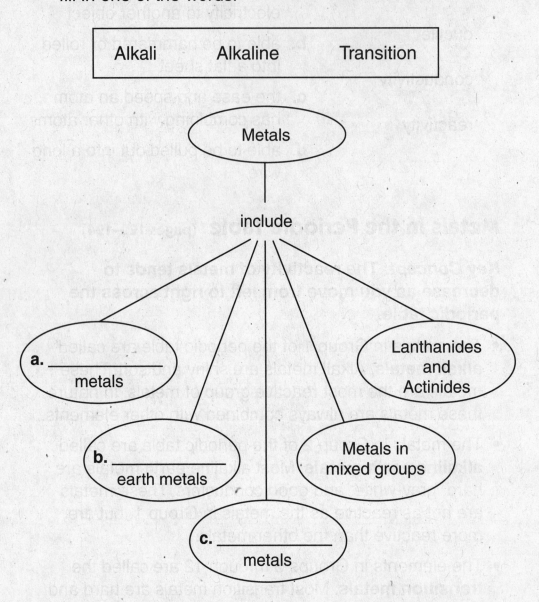

| Alkali | Alkaline | Transition |
|---|---|---|

Metals

include

a. _____ metals

b. _____ earth metals

c. _____ metals

Metals in mixed groups

Lanthanides and Actinides

5. Is the following sentence true or false? Metals in Group 1 are the most reactive metals. _____

# Synthetic Elements (pages 124–125)

***Key Concept:* Elements that follow uranium are made—or synthesized—when nuclear particles are forced to crash into one another.**

- Elements with atomic numbers higher than 92 are not found naturally on Earth. These heavier elements were made by scientists in a laboratory.

- Scientists use machines called particle accelerators to make these heavier elements. **Particle accelerators** are machines that move the nucleus of an atom faster and faster. As the nucleus moves faster, it gains energy. If the nucleus of an atom has enough energy when it crashes into the nucleus of another atom, then the two nuclei will join to form one larger nucleus.

*Answer the following questions. Use your textbook and the ideas above.*

6. Is the following sentence true or false? Elements with atomic numbers higher that 92 are found naturally on Earth. _____

7. A particle accelerator is a machine that is used to
   a. slow atoms down.
   b. make heavier elements.
   c. measure the reactivity of metals.

**Elements and the Periodic Table**

# Nonmetals and Metalloids
(pages 128–135)

## Properties of Nonmetals (pages 129–130)

*Key Concept:* **Most nonmetals are poor conductors of electricity and heat and are reactive with other elements. Solid nonmetals are dull and brittle.**

- A **nonmetal** is any element that is not a metal. Most nonmetals are gases.

- The physical properties of nonmetals are the opposite of the physical properties of metals. Nonmetals are not shiny. Solid nonmetals break apart easily when hammered. Nonmetals do not move heat or electricity to other objects.

- The chemical properties of nonmetals are also the opposite of the chemical properties of metals. The atoms of nonmetals usually react with the atoms of other elements by gaining electrons or sharing electrons. Most nonmetals react very easily with the atoms of other elements.

*Answer the following question. Use your textbook and the ideas above.*

1. For each property listed, write *P* if the property describes a physical property of nonmetals. Write *C* if the property describes a chemical property of nonmetals.

   **a.** very reactive _____

   **b.** not shiny _____

   **c.** break apart easily _____

   **d.** gain or share electrons _____

   **e.** do not move heat to other objects _____

# Families of Nonmetals (pages 130–134)

*Key Concept:* **Beginning with the nonmetal in Group 14, nonmetals gain or share fewer electrons as you move right across the periodic table. Elements in Group 18 do not usually gain or share any electrons.**

- Carbon is the only nonmetal in Group 14. Carbon shares or loses four electrons when it reacts with the atoms of other elements.

- Nitrogen and phosphorus are the two nonmetals in Group 15. Nitrogen and phosphorus gain or share three electrons when reacting with the atoms of other elements.

- Oxygen, sulfur, and selenium are the nonmetals in Group 16. These elements gain or share two electrons when reacting with atoms of other elements.

- The elements in Group 17 are called the **halogens**. All the elements in Group 17, except one, are nonmetals. The atoms of halogens gain or share one electron when reacting with the atoms of other elements. All the halogens are very reactive.

- The elements in Group 18 are called the **noble gases**. All elements in Group 18 are nonmetals, and all are gases. The atoms of noble gases do not usually gain, share, or lose electrons. Noble gases do not form compounds with other elements.

*Answer the following questions. Use your textbook and the ideas above.*

**2.** As you move to the right across the periodic table, beginning with Group 16, nonmetals

   **a.** lose more electrons.

   **b.** gain or share fewer electrons.

   **c.** gain or share more electrons.

**Elements and the Periodic Table**

3. Read each word in the box. In each sentence below, fill in the correct word or words.

| metals | halogens | noble gases |

a. Elements that are gases and do not usually gain or share any electrons are the

_____.

b. Elements in Group 17 gain or share one electron and are called the _____.

## The Metalloids (page 135)

*Key Concept:* **The most useful property of the metalloids is their varying ability to conduct electricity.**

- **Metalloids** are elements that have some properties of metals and some properties of nonmetals. Metalloids are found in the periodic table along the zigzag line between the metals and the nonmetals.

- All metalloids are solids. Metalloids break easily, are hard, and somewhat reactive.

- Metalloids can move electricity to other objects only at certain temperatures or in certain amounts of light. Because of this property, metalloids are good semiconductors. A **semiconductor** is a material that can move electricity in some conditions but not in other conditions. Semiconductors are used in computers and lasers.

**Elements and the Periodic Table**

*Answer the following questions. Use your textbook and the ideas on page 64.*

4. Metalloids are elements that have properties of

   a. both metals and nonmetals.

   b. neither metals nor nonmetals.

   c. only gases.

5. Look at the diagram of the periodic table below. Color in the boxes for elements that are metalloids. You may use the periodic table in your book.

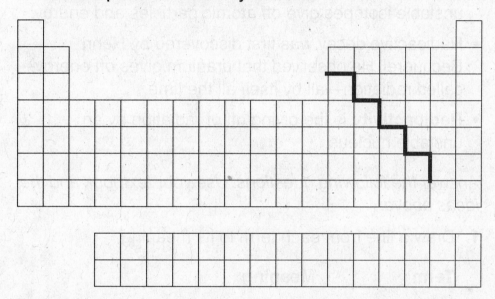

6. A material that can move electricity in some conditions but not in other conditions is called a

   a. metal.

   b. noble gas.

   c. semiconductor.

# Radioactive Elements (pages 138–143)

## Radioactivity (page 139)

*Key Concept:* **In 1896, the French scientist Henri Becquerel discovered the effects of radioactive decay quite by accident while studying a mineral containing uranium.**

- Some isotopes of elements break apart naturally. **Radioactive decay** is a process in which the nuclei of unstable isotopes give off atomic particles and energy.

- Radioactive decay was first discovered by Henri Becquerel. He observed that uranium gives off energy—called radiation—all by itself all the time.

- **Radioactivity** is the giving off of radiation by an unstable nucleus.

*Answer the following questions. Use your textbook and the ideas above.*

1. Draw a line from each term to its meaning.

| Term | Meaning |
|------|---------|
| radioactive decay | **a.** the giving off of radiation by an unstable nucleus |
| radioactivity | **b.** the process in which nuclei give off atomic particles and energy |

2. Is the following sentence true or false? Henri Becquerel discovered radioactive decay by accident. _____

# Types of Radioactive Decay (pages 140–141)

*Key Concept:* **Natural radioactive decay can produce alpha particles, beta particles, and gamma rays.**

- The three forms of radiation are alpha particles, beta particles, and gamma radiation.

- An **alpha particle** is made up of two protons and two neutrons. When an atom releases an alpha particle, the atom's atomic number decreases by 2. The atom has become a different element.

- A **beta particle** is a fast-moving electron given off by a nucleus. A beta particle forms when an unstable neutron changes into a proton and an electron. The proton stays in the nucleus, and the electron is the beta particle. The atomic number of the atom increases by 1. The atom is a different element.

- **Gamma radiation** is the energy that is released in a nuclear reaction. Whenever an alpha particle or a beta particle is released, gamma radiation is also released. The release of gamma radiation does not change the atomic number of an atom.

*Answer the following questions. Use your textbook and the ideas above.*

3. Circle the letter of the form of radiation that does NOT change the atomic number of an atom.
    a. alpha particle
    b. beta particle
    c. gamma radiation

4. Is the following sentence true of false? When an atom releases a beta particle, the atom has become a different element. _____

**Elements and the Periodic Table**

5. The picture shows radioactive decay in which an alpha particle is produced. Circle the alpha particle.

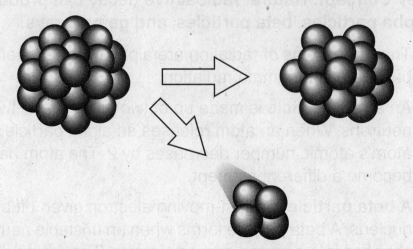

6. After releasing the alpha particle, how has the atom changed? Circle the letter of the correct answer.

   a. The atom has not changed.

   b. The atomic number of the atom has decreased by 2.

   c. The atomic number of the atom has increased by 2.

## Using Radioactive Isotopes (pages 141–143)

*Key Concept:* **Uses of radioactive isotopes include tracing the steps of chemical reactions and industrial processes, and diagnosing and treating disease.**

- Radioactive isotopes have many uses in science and industry.

- Because radiation can be observed, a radioactive isotope can be used to follow the steps of a process. **Tracers** are radioactive isotopes used to trace the steps of a chemical reaction or industrial process.

**Elements and the Periodic Table**

- In industry, tracers are used to find weak spots in metal pipes. Tracers can be easily observed if they leak out of the pipes.

- Doctors use radioactive isotopes to find medical problems in a patient. Doctors inject traces into a patient and then observe how the tracers move through the body's organs.

- Doctors also treat some diseases with radioactive isotopes. In a process called radiation therapy, radioactive elements are used to destroy unhealthy cells. Radiation therapy is often used to destroy cancer cells.

*Answer the following questions. Use your textbook and the ideas on page 68 and above.*

7. Radioactive isotopes used to trace the steps of a process are called _____.

8. Circle the letter of each sentence that is true about using radioactive isotopes.

   a. Doctors use radioactive isotopes to find medical problems in a patient.

   b. Doctors use radioactive isotopes to find leaks in medical machines.

   c. Industry uses radioactive isotopes to find weak spots in metal pipes.

**Atoms and Bonding**

# Atoms, Bonding, and the Periodic Table (pages 150–156)

## Valence Electrons and Bonding (pages 150–151)

*Key Concept:* The number of valence electrons in an atom of an element determines many properties of that element, including the ways in which the atom can bond with other atoms.

- The **valence** (VAY luns) **electrons** of an atom are the electrons in the highest energy level. These electrons are far away from the pull of the nucleus. So, an atom easily loses valence electrons.

- An **electron dot diagram** shows the number of valence electrons for an element. Each dot in the diagram stands for one valence electron. An element can have from one to eight valence electrons.

- Most atoms are stable when they have eight valence electrons. When atoms are stable, they do not react with other atoms.

- When some atoms react, they gain electrons from another atom to increase their number of valence electrons to eight. Other atoms give up their valence electrons.

- When atoms lose, share, or gain electrons, the atoms react, or join together chemically. A **chemical bond** is the pulling force between two atoms that holds them together.

*Answer the following questions. Use your textbook and the ideas above.*

1. Is the following sentence true or false? The valence electrons of an atom are the electrons in the lowest energy level closest to the nucleus. _____

**2.** Look at the electron dot diagrams for sodium (Na), carbon (C), and oxygen (O). Draw a line from each element to its number of valence electrons.

| Element | Number of Valence Electrons |
|---|---|
| Na· | **a.** 6 |
| ·Ċ· | **b.** 4 |
| ·Ö: | **c.** 1 |

**3.** Circle the letter of each sentence that is true.

**a.** Atoms with eight valence electrons easily react with other atoms.

**b.** Atoms lose or gain electrons when they react with other atoms.

**c.** When atoms form chemical bonds with other atoms, the atoms have joined together chemically.

## How the Periodic Table Works (pages 152–156)

*Key Concept:* **The periodic table gives you information about the arrangement of electrons in atoms. The elements within a group have similar properties because they all have the same number of valence electrons in their atoms.**

- The periodic table shows the elements arranged in a certain way. The arrangement of elements tells you which elements will combine and how.

- As you look across a period, or row, you can see that the atomic numbers increase from left to right. As the atomic number increases, the number of electrons also increases. This pattern is the same for every period. This pattern means that the elements within a group always have the same number of valence electrons.

**Atoms and Bonding**

- Most of the elements of Group 18—the noble gases—have eight valence electrons. Atoms with eight valence electrons are unlikely to give up electrons to other atoms. As a result, the noble gases do not react easily with other elements.

- Elements of Group 1 react very easily. They can become stable by losing just one valence electron. Elements of Group 17 also react very easily. They can become stable by gaining just one electron.

- How reactive a metal is depends on how easily its atoms lose valence electrons. Among Groups 1 and 2, reactivity increases from top to bottom.

- Elements in the green section of the periodic table are the nonmetals. Most nonmetals are gases at room temperature.

- Metalloids lie along a zigzag line between the metals and nonmetals. These elements can behave as either metals or nonmetals.

- Hydrogen is located in Group 1, but it is considered to be a nonmetal.

*Answer the following questions. Use your textbook and the ideas on page 71 and above.*

4. Circle the letter of why elements within a group on the periodic table have similar properties.

   a. They all have the same number of neutrons in their atoms.

   b. They all have the same number of valence electrons in their atoms.

   c. They all can behave as metals or nonmetals.

5. Is the following sentence true or false? How reactive a metal is depends on how easily its atoms lose valence electrons. _____

# Ionic Bonds (pages 158–163)

## Ions and Ionic Bonds (pages 159–160)

**Key Concept:** When an atom loses an electron, it loses a negative charge and becomes a positive ion. When an atom gains an electron, it gains a negative charge and becomes a negative ion. Ionic bonds form as a result of the attraction between positive and negative ions.

- An atom with an electric charge is called an **ion** (EYE ahn). An atom does not have an electric charge unless it loses or gains an electron.

- If an atom loses an electron, it has more protons. So, the atom becomes an ion with a positive electric charge. If an atom gains an electron, it has more electrons. The atom becomes an ion with a negative electric charge.

- An **ionic bond** is the attraction between a positive ion and a negative ion.

- A compound that is made up of positive and negative ions is called an **ionic compound**.

*Answer the following questions. Use your textbook and the ideas above.*

1. Read each word in the box. In each sentence below, fill in the correct word or words.

| ion | ionic bond | valence electron |
|-----|-----------|------------------|

a. The attraction between a positive ion and a negative ion is a(an) _____.

b. An atom with an electric charge is called a(an)

_____.

**Atoms and Bonding**

2. The picture shows how sodium atoms join with chlorine atoms to form sodium chloride. Circle the ionic compound.

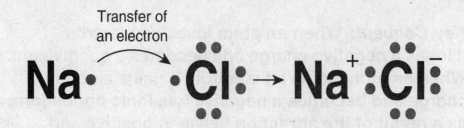

Transfer of
an electron

3. In the picture above, which atom lost an electron to become a positive ion? Circle the letter of the correct answer.

   **a.** Na       **b.** Cl       **c.** NaCl

## Chemical Formulas and Names (page 161)

*Key Concept:* **When ionic compounds form, the ions come together in a way that balances out the charges on the ions. The chemical formula for the compound reflects this balance. For an ionic compound, the name of the positive ion comes first, followed by the name of the negative ion.**

- A **chemical formula** is a group of symbols that shows how much of each element is in a compound. A **subscript** tells you the ratio of elements in the compound. For $MgCl_2$, there are two chloride (Cl) ions for every one magnesium (Mg) ion.

- When an ionic compound forms, the ions join so that the electric charges equal zero. When magnesium chloride ($MgCl_2$) forms, two chloride ions of 1− are needed to balance the 2+ charge of a magnesium ion.

- When an ionic compound is named, the positive ion comes first. The negative ion is the second part of the name. For magnesium chloride ($MgCl_2$), magnesium (Mg) is the positive ion and chloride (Cl) is the negative ion.

**Atoms and Bonding**

*Answer the following questions. Use your textbook and the ideas on page 74.*

**4.** Read each word in the box. In each sentence below, fill in the correct word or words.

| | | |
|---|---|---|
| chemical formula | ionic compound | subscript |

  **a.** A number that tells you the ratio of elements in a compound is a(an) _____.

  **b.** A group of symbols that shows the elements in a compound is a(an) _____.

**5.** Circle the letter of each sentence that is true about ionic compounds.

  **a.** When an ionic compound forms, the ions join so that the electric charges equal zero.

  **b.** $MgCl_2$ has two ions of Mg.

  **c.** When naming ionic compounds, the negative ion comes first.

## Properties of Ionic Compounds (pages 162–163)

*Key Concepts:* **In general, ionic compounds are hard, brittle crystals that have high melting points. When dissolved in water or melted, they conduct electricity.**

- When ions join together to form ionic compounds, the positive ions are always surrounded by negative ions on all sides. The positive and negative ions form an orderly pattern called a **crystal**.

- Many crystals of ionic compounds are hard and break easily. The crystals have these properties because ionic bonds are very strong.

**Atoms and Bonding**

- Crystals of ionic compounds have high melting points. A lot of heat is needed to give ions enough energy to break away from each other.

- When ionic compounds dissolve in water, the solution can conduct electricity. Crystals of ionic compounds cannot conduct electricity.

*Answer the following questions. Use your textbook and the ideas on page 75 and above.*

**6.** Read each word in the box. Use the words to complete the concept map about ionic compounds.

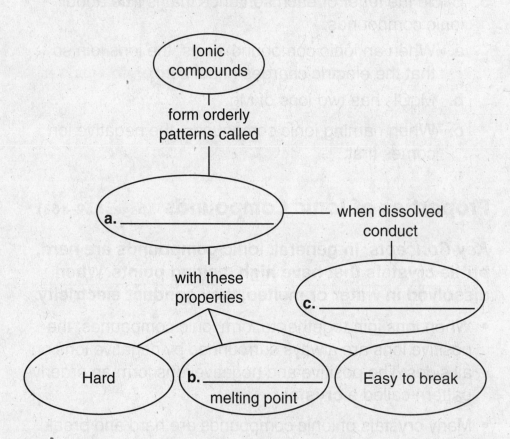

Crystals    Electricity    High    Low

Ionic compounds

form orderly patterns called

a. _____

when dissolved conduct

c. _____

with these properties

Hard

b. _____ melting point

Easy to break

**7.** Is the following sentence true or false? Ionic bonds are very strong. _____

**Atoms and Bonding**

# Covalent Bonds (pages 166–171)

## How Covalent Bonds Form (pages 167–168)

*Key Concept:* **The force that holds atoms together in a covalent bond is the attraction of each atom's nucleus for the shared pair of electrons.**

- Atoms can become more stable by sharing electrons. A **covalent bond** is a chemical bond that forms when two atoms share electrons.

- When an atom shares an electron with another atom, neither atom loses an electron or gains an electron. The positive electric charge of the nucleus of each atom holds the shared electrons in place. Both atoms have a stable set of eight electrons.

- A group of atoms with no electric charge that are joined by covalent bonds is a **molecule**.

- The number of covalent bonds an atom can form depends on its number of valence electrons. Oxygen, for example, has six valence electrons. Oxygen needs two more electrons to have a set of eight valence electrons. Oxygen can form two covalent bonds.

- Two atoms can share more than one pair of electrons. A **double bond** forms when two atoms share two pairs of electrons. A **triple bond** forms when two atoms share three pairs of electrons.

*Answer the following questions. Use your textbook and the ideas above.*

**1.** Is the following sentence true or false? A covalent bond

forms when two atoms share electrons. _____

**Atoms and Bonding**

**2.** The picture shows the formation of a covalent bond between two fluorine (F) atoms. Circle the shared electrons.

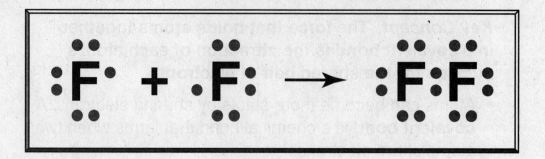

**3.** Draw a line from each term to its meaning.

| Term | Meaning |
|------|---------|
| molecule | **a.** bond that forms when two atoms share two pairs of electrons |
| double bond | **b.** a group of atoms with no electric charge that are joined by covalent bonds |
| triple bond | **c.** bond that forms when two atoms share three pairs of electrons |

**Atoms and Bonding**

# Molecular Compounds (pages 168–169)

*Key Concept:* **Compared to ionic compounds, molecular compounds generally have lower melting points and boiling points, and they do not conduct electricity when dissolved in water.**

- A **molecular compound** is a compound that is made up of molecules. Water is a molecular compound. Table sugar is also a molecular compound.

- Covalent bonds hold the atoms of molecules close together. But covalent bonds are not as strong as ionic bonds.

- Compared to ionic compounds, less heat is needed to melt a solid molecular compound. Molecular compounds are often liquids or gases at room temperature.

- Most molecular compounds do not conduct electricity. Molecular compounds do not have any charged particles, so electricity cannot flow.

*Answer the following questions. Use your textbook and the ideas above.*

4. A compound that is made up of molecules is called

   a(an) _____ compound.

5. Circle the letter of each sentence that is true about molecular compounds.

   a. Covalent bonds are stronger than ionic bonds.

   b. Compared to ionic compounds, more heat is needed to melt a solid molecular compound.

   c. Molecular compounds do not conduct electricity.

# Unequal Sharing of Electrons (pages 169–171)

*Key Concept:* **Atoms of some elements pull more strongly on shared electrons than do atoms of other elements. As a result, the electrons are pulled more toward one atom, causing the bonded atoms to have slight electrical charges.**

- Sometimes one atom in a covalent bond pulls more strongly on the shared electrons than the other atom. When this happens, the electrons are no longer equally shared. So, the atom that is pulling the electron pair closer to it has a slightly negative charge. The atom that has a weaker hold on the electron pair has a slightly positive charge.

- A **polar bond** is a covalent bond in which the electrons are not equally shared. The covalent bond between an oxygen atom and a hydrogen atom is a polar bond.

- Not all covalent bonds are polar bonds. If the atoms are the same size, such as two fluorine atoms, then the electrons are pulled equally by the nucleus of each atom. A **nonpolar bond** is a covalent bond in which the electrons are shared equally.

*Answer the following questions. Use your textbook and the ideas above.*

6. Is the following sentence true or false? The electrons in a covalent bond are always equally shared.

   _____

7. Circle the letter of a covalent bond in which the electrons are equally shared.

   a. polar bond

   b. nonpolar bond

   c. ionic bond

# Bonding in Metals (pages 172–177)

## Metals and Alloys (page 173)

*Key Concept:* **Alloys are generally stronger and less likely to react with air or water than are the pure metals from which they are made.**

- An **alloy** is a mixture of two or more elements, and at least one element is a metal.

- The properties of an alloy are different than the properties of the elements it is made of. For example, pure gold is very soft and easily bent. Gold mixed with copper or silver is much harder. Gold alloys are used for jewelry.

- Alloys are stronger than pure metals. Alloys do not rust as easily are pure metals.

*Answer the following questions. Use your textbook and the ideas above.*

1. A mixture of a metal with another element is called a(an)
   a. polymer.
   b. composite.
   c. alloy.

2. Is the following sentence true or false? Pure metals are usually stronger than alloys. _____

# Metallic Bonding (page 174)

*Key Concept:* **A metal or metal alloy consists of positively charged metal ions embedded in a "sea" of valence electrons.**

- The physical and chemical properties of metals or metal alloys can be explained by the structure of metal atoms and by the bonding between them.

- Most metals have one, two, or three valence electrons. Metals easily lose electrons. Metal ions have a positive electric charge.

- Solid metals are crystals. Metal atoms in the crystal are very close together. The atoms in a metal crystal are arranged in a specific way.

- In a metal crystal, the atoms exist as positive ions. The valence electrons lost from the ions freely drift around the ions in the crystal. The metal ions are held in place by metallic bonds. A **metallic bond** is the attraction between a positive metal ion and the electrons around it.

*Answer the following questions. Use your textbook and the ideas above.*

3. Circle the letter of an attraction between a positive metal ion and the electrons around it.

    **a.** ionic bond

    **b.** covalent bond

    **c.** metallic bond

4. Circle the letter of each sentence that is true about metallic bonding.

    **a.** Most metals have one, two, or three valence electrons.

    **b.** Metals easily lose protons.

    **c.** Metal ions have a positive electrical charge.

**Atoms and Bonding**

# Metallic Properties (pages 175–177)

*Key Concept:* The "sea of electrons" model of solid metals explains the ease with which they can change shape, their ability to conduct electric current, their luster, and their ability to conduct heat.

- You can easily change the shape of a metal because the metal ions are not attracted to other ions. The ions are attracted only to the loose valence electrons around them. So, the ions can be pushed out of position.

- Because metal ions move easily, metals are ductile. Ductile means that a metal can be bent easily and pulled into a wire. Metals are malleable, too. Malleable means that a metal can be rolled into thin sheets or beaten into a shape.

- Electric current is possible when charged particles are free to move. Because the electrons in metals are free to move, metals conduct current easily.

- When light strikes valence electrons, the electrons absorb the light and then give it off again. This makes metals look shiny.

- Heat causes particles to move faster. In metals, the valence electrons are free to move. The electrons in the warmer parts of the metal transfer energy to particles in the cooler parts of the metal.

*Answer the following questions. Use your textbook and the ideas above.*

5. Is the following sentence true or false? Heat flows easily through metals because the positive metal ions are free to move. _____

Name _____ Date _____ Class _____

**Atoms and Bonding**

6. Look at the pictures of the paper clip and the aluminum pan. Circle the picture that shows that metal is ductile.

7. Read each word in the box. Use the words to complete the concept map about metals.

| Ductile | Heat | Luster | Malleable |
|---------|------|--------|-----------|

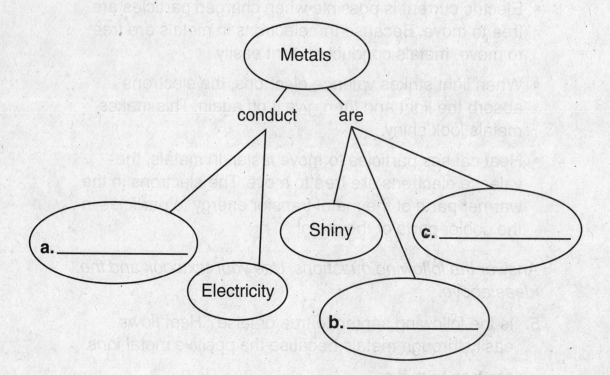

# Observing Chemical Change

(pages 184–191)

## Properties and Changes of Matter

(pages 185–187)

*Key Concept:* **Matter can be described in terms of two kinds of properties—physical properties and chemical properties. Changes in matter can be described in terms of physical changes and chemical changes. Chemical changes occur when bonds break and new bonds form.**

- A **physical property** is anything that you can see, smell, feel, taste, or hear about a substance.

- Some physical properties are color, hardness, and shine. Melting temperature and being able to conduct electricity are also physical properties.

- A **chemical property** tells how a substance changes to another substance. One chemical property is being able to react with other elements.

- A **physical change** is a change in the way a substance looks. The substance is still the same substance. Changing from water to ice is a physical change. Bending, crushing, and cutting are also physical changes.

- A **chemical reaction** is a chemical change. A chemical reaction is a change in matter that produces one or more new substances. Burning gasoline in a car's engine is a chemical change.

- New substances form in a chemical reaction because the chemical bonds between atoms break. Then the atoms form new bonds between different atoms. The new substances are made up of a different combination of atoms and have different properties.

Chemical Reactions

**Chemical Reactions**

*Answer the following questions. Use your textbook and the ideas on page 85.*

1. Circle the letter of a characteristic that describes how a substance can change to another substance.
   a. physical property
   b. chemical property
   c. physical change

2. Look at the pictures of the burning candle and the melting ice cube. Label the physical change and the chemical change.

   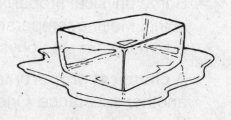

a. _____   b. _____

3. Is the following sentence true or false? When a chemical reaction occurs, the bonds of a substance break and new bonds form. _____

# Evidence for Chemical Reactions (pages 188–191)

*Key Concept:* **Chemical reactions involve two main kinds of changes that you can observe—formation of new substances and changes in energy.**

- You can tell that a chemical reaction has occurred when you observe that a new substance has formed.

- A new substance has formed when the properties have changed. For example, a solid forms when two liquids are mixed.

- Changes in energy are also signs of a chemical reaction. In an **endothermic** (en doh THUR mik) **reaction**, energy is absorbed. Frying an egg is an endothermic reaction. You must keep adding heat, or the reaction will stop.

- An **exothermic** (ek soh THUR mik) **reaction** is a reaction that gives off energy in the form of heat. Burning wood is an exothermic reaction because heat is given off.

*Answer the following questions. Use your textbook and the ideas on page 86 and above.*

4. Circle the letter of each sentence that is true about chemical reactions.

   a. New substances form during chemical reactions.

   b. A solid forming when two liquids are mixed is a sign that a chemical reaction has occurred.

   c. Changes in energy never occur during chemical reactions.

5. Fill in the table about changes in energy in chemical reactions.

| Energy Changes in Chemical Reactions | | |
|---|---|---|
| **Type of Reaction** | **Energy Change** | **Example** |
| Endothermic | energy is a. _____ | frying an egg |
| b. _____ | energy is given off | burning wood |

**Chemical Reactions**

# Describing Chemical Reactions (pages 194–201)

## What Are Chemical Equations? (page 195)

*Key Concept:* Chemical equations use chemical formulas and other symbols instead of words to summarize a reaction.

- A **chemical equation** uses symbols to show a chemical reaction in a short, easy way.

- All chemical equations use chemical formulas for the substances in a reaction. For example, the chemical formula for water is $H_2O$.

- Chemical equations show the substances you begin with and the substances that form at the end. **Reactants** are the substances you begin with. **Products** are the new substances formed in the reaction.

- The general form for a chemical equation is:

  Reactant + Reactant → Product + Product

  Read the arrow as "yields," which means "forms" or "gives."

- The number of reactants and products can be different. Reactions might have only one reactant or one product. Other reactions might have two or more reactants or products.

*Answer the following questions. Use your textbook and the ideas above.*

1. Look at the chemical equation below. Circle the reactant.

$$CaCO_3 \rightarrow CaO + CO_2$$

**Chemical Reactions**

2. Circle the letter of how many products are formed in the reaction in question 1.

   **a.** 1

   **b.** 2

   **c.** 3

# Conservation of Mass (pages 196–197)

*Key Concept:* **The principle of conservation of mass states that in a chemical reaction, the total mass of the reactants must equal the total mass of the products.**

- The principle of **conservation of mass** states that during a chemical reaction, matter is not created or destroyed. All the atoms present at the start of the reaction are also present at the end of the reaction. So, the products and the reactants have the same number of atoms.

- Some reactions, like burning wood, do not seem to follow the principle of conservation of mass. However, when wood burns, some of the products escape into the air.

*Answer the following questions. Use your textbook and the ideas above.*

3. What principle states that during a chemical reaction, matter is not created or destroyed?

   _____

4. Is the following sentence true or false? Matter is not created or destroyed in a chemical reaction.

   _____

5. The products of a chemical reaction always have the same number of _____ as the reactants.

Chemical Reactions

# Balancing Chemical Equations
(pages 198–199)

*Key Concept:* **To describe a reaction accurately, a chemical equation must show the same number of each type of atom on both sides of the equation.**

- Chemical equations must show the same number of atoms for the products and the reactants. Then the equation is balanced.

- To balance a chemical equation, first write the equation. Then count the atoms of each element on both sides of the equation. If the number of atoms is not equal, then the equation is not balanced.

- Balance the equation by adding a coefficient. A **coefficient** (koh uh FISH unt) is a number placed in front of a chemical formula in an equation. The coefficient tells you how many atoms or molecules of a reactant or a product are in the reaction.

- Finally, check the equation. Count the atoms on both sides of the equation again. If the number of atoms on both sides of the equation is equal, the equation is balanced.

*Answer the following questions. Use your textbook and the ideas above.*

6. Is the following sentence true or false? In the chemical equation $Mg + O_2 \rightarrow MgO$, both sides of the equation have the same number of oxygen atoms. _____

7. For each chemical equation below, fill in the correct number to balance the equation.

   a. _____ $H_2 + O_2 \rightarrow 2H_2O$

   b. $2 NaN_3 \rightarrow 2 Na + $ _____ $N_2$

# Classifying Chemical Reactions (pages 200–201)

*Key Concept:* **Many chemical equations can be classified in one of three categories: synthesis, decomposition, or replacement.**

- In a **synthesis** (SIN thuh sis) reaction, two or more elements or compounds combine and make a new, more complex product. The reaction of hydrogen and oxygen to make water is a synthesis reaction.

$$2H_2 + O_2 \rightarrow 2\,H_2O$$

- In a **decomposition** (dee KAHM puh zih shun) reaction, compounds are broken down into simpler products. For example, hydrogen peroxide breaks down to water and oxygen.

$$2\,H_2O_2 \rightarrow 2\,H_2O + O_2$$

- In a **replacement** reaction, one element replaces another element in a compound. For example, copper metal is the product when copper oxide is heated with carbon.

$$2\,Cu_2O + C \rightarrow 4\,Cu + CO_2$$

This is a single replacement reaction because only one element, carbon, replaces another element, Cu, in the reaction.

*Answer the following questions. Use your textbook and the ideas above.*

**8.** The three categories of chemical equations are synthesis, decomposition, and

_____.

**Chemical Reactions**

9. Draw a line from each term to the chemical reaction that is an example of the term.

**Term**

synthesis

decomposition

replacement

**Example**

a. $2 Cu_2O + C \rightarrow 4 Cu + CO_2$

b. $2H_2 + O_2 \rightarrow 2 H_2O$

c. $2 H_2O_2 \rightarrow 2 H_2O + O_2$

10. Fill in the blanks in the concept map about kinds of chemical reactions.

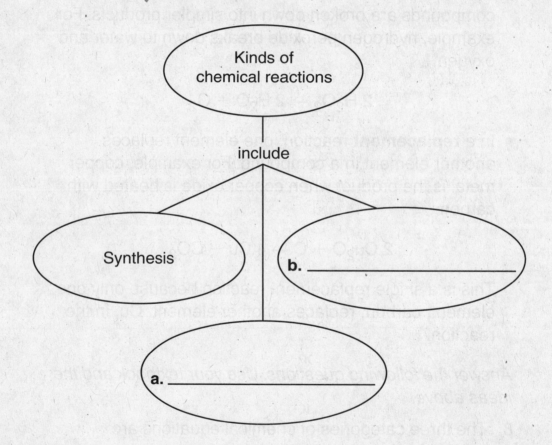

**Chemical Reactions**

# Controlling Chemical Reactions (pages 204–209)

## Energy and Reactions (pages 205–206)

*Key Concepts:* **All chemical reactions need a certain amount of activation energy to get started.**

- **Activation energy** is the smallest amount of energy needed to start a chemical reaction.

- All chemical reactions need a little energy to get started. This energy is used to break the chemical bonds of the reactants. Then, the atoms begin to form the chemical bonds of the products.

- In exothermic reactions, the products have less energy than the reactants. As a result, the reaction gives off heat energy.

- Endothermic reactions need activation energy plus energy to keep the reaction going. As a result, energy must be added to the reaction.

*Answer the following questions. Use your textbook and the ideas above.*

1. Circle the letter of each sentence that is true about activation energy.

   a. All chemical reactions need activation energy.

   b. Exothermic reactions do not need activation energy.

   c. Endothermic reactions need activation energy and energy to keep going.

**Chemical Reactions**

2. Look at the graphs below. Circle the letter of the graph in which the products have less energy than the reactants.

a.

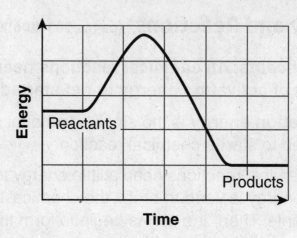

b.

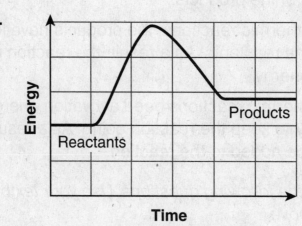

3. Draw a line from each term to its meaning.

| Term | Meaning |
|------|---------|
| activation energy | **a.** the products have more energy than the reactants |
| endothermic reaction | **b.** the products have less energy than the reactants |
| exothermic reaction | **c.** required to start a chemical reaction |

**Chemical Reactions**

# Rates of Chemical Reactions (pages 207–209)

***Key Concept:*** **Chemists can control rates of reactions by changing factors such as surface area, temperature, and concentration, and by using substances called catalysts and inhibitors.**

- Chemical reactions do not all occur at the same rate. Some reactions, like explosions, are very fast. Other reactions, like rusting metal, are very slow.

- Chemists can speed up reactions or slow them down. One way to speed up a reaction is to increase the surface area. When you break a solid into small pieces, more particles can react at once.

- Chemists also increase temperature to speed up a reaction. At higher temperatures, particles move faster and have more chances to react. Chemical bonds also break more easily. At lower temperatures, reactions slow down.

- **Concentration** is the amount of a substance in a given volume. Increasing the concentration of the reactants speeds up a reaction. More particles can react at once.

- A **catalyst** (KAT uh list) is a material that increases the speed of a reaction by lowering the activation energy. A catalyst does this by bringing the reactants close together. A catalyst is not changed in a reaction, so a catalyst is not a reactant.

- An **inhibitor** is a material used to slow down a reaction. Most inhibitors work by keeping reactants away from each other.

*Answer the following questions. Use your textbook and the ideas above.*

**4.** Is the following sentence true or false? All chemical

reactions occur at the same speed. _____

**Chemical Reactions**

5. Complete the table. Write *F* if the chemical reaction will go faster. Write *S* if the chemical reaction will slow down.

| Controlling Speeds of Chemical Reactions | |
| --- | --- |
| **Reaction Conditions** | **Reaction Occurs Faster or Slower?** |
| Surface area increases | **a.** _____ |
| Temperature increases | **b.** _____ |
| Temperature decreases | **c.** _____ |
| Concentration increases | **d.** _____ |

6. Draw a line from each term to its meaning.

**Term**

concentration

catalyst

inhibitor

**Meaning**

**a.** a material that slows down a reaction

**b.** a material that speeds up a reaction

**c.** the amount of a substance in a given volume

Chemical Reactions

# Fire and Fire Safety (pages 212–215)

## Understanding Fire (pages 213–214)

*Key Concept:* **The following three things are necessary to start and maintain a fire—fuel, oxygen, and heat.**

- Fire is caused by combustion. **Combustion** is a very fast reaction between oxygen and a fuel. A **fuel** is a material that gives off energy when it burns. Oil, wood, and gasoline are fuels.

- A fire cannot start unless there is fuel, oxygen, and heat. Oxygen comes from the air. Heat gives the activation energy needed to start combustion. The heat from a lighted match or an electric spark can start a fire.

- A fire will continue to burn as long as it has fuel, oxygen, and heat.

- Firefighters put out fires by removing fuel, oxygen, or heat. Water covers the fuel and keeps it from getting oxygen from the air. The evaporation of water uses a lot of heat, causing the fire to cool. Without heat, there is not enough energy to keep combustion going. The fire goes out.

*Answer the following questions. Use your textbook and the ideas above.*

1. A material that releases energy when it burns is

   called a(an) _____.

2. A very fast reaction between oxygen and a fuel is

   called _____.

**3.** Look at the fire triangle. Then circle the letter of what is missing from the fire triangle.

a. Catalyst

b. Inhibitor

c. Heat

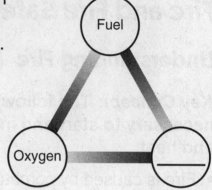

## Home Fire Safety (pages 214–215)

*Key Concept:* **If you know how to prevent fires in your home and what to do if a fire starts, you are better prepared to take action.**

- You can control a small fire by using the fire triangle. You can smother a fire, or keep the fire from getting oxygen.

- A small fire is easy to control. You can cool a match just by blowing on it.

- A fire that is growing as you fight it is out of control. Get away from the fire and call the fire department.

- The best way to stop a fire is to prevent one from starting. Store items that burn easily in places far from sources of flames.

*Answer the following question. Use your textbook and the ideas above.*

**4.** Circle the letter of each sentence that is true about fire safety.

a. You can smother a fire by getting oxygen to it.

b. If a fire gets out of control, you should call the fire department.

c. The best way to stop a fire is to prevent one from starting.

# Understanding Solutions (pages 222–227)

## What Is a Solution? (pages 222–223)

*Key Concept:* **A solution has the same properties throughout. It contains solute particles (molecules or ions) that are too small to see.**

- A **solution** is a well-mixed mixture. In a solution, you cannot see the separate parts of the mixture. All samples of a solution have the same properties. Tree sap is a solution. Soft drinks are solutions, too.

- A solution has two parts. The **solvent** is the largest part of a solution. The solvent dissolves the other parts of a solution. Water is the solvent in soft drinks and tree sap.

- The **solute** is the smaller part of a solution. The solute is dissolved by the solvent. Sugar is one of the solutes in soft drinks and tree sap.

- Many solutions are not made of liquids. Air is a mixture of gases. Brass is a mixture of solids.

*Answer the following questions. Use your textbook and the ideas above.*

1. Draw a line from each term to its meaning.

| Term | Meaning |
|------|---------|
| solution | **a.** the largest part of the solution |
| solvent | **b.** the smaller part of a solution |
| solute | **c.** a well-mixed mixture |

2. Is the following sentence true or false? Air is an example of a solution. _____

Acids, Bases, and Solutions

# Colloids and Suspensions (page 224)

*Key Concept:* **A colloid contains larger particles than a solution. A suspension has even larger particles and does not have the same properties throughout.**

- A **colloid** (KAHL oyd) is a mixture that contains small, undissolved particles that do not settle out. Examples of colloids are gelatin, milk, and fog.

- The particles in a colloid are too small to be seen. However, the particles in a colloid are big enough to scatter light. You cannot see clearly through a colloid.

- A **suspension** (suh SPEN shun) is a mixture in which the particles are big enough to see. An example of a suspension is orange juice with pulp.

- Because the particles in a suspension are so large, the particles are easy to remove by filtering or by letting them settle out.

*Answer the following questions. Use your textbook and the ideas above.*

3. Read each word in the box. In each sentence below, fill in one of the words.

| colloid | solution | suspension |
|---|---|---|

   a. A mixture in which the particles are big enough to see is a _____.

   b. A mixture that contains small, undissolved particles that do not settle out is a _____.

4. Circle the letter of the kind of mixture that has the largest particles.

   a. solution     b. colloid     c. suspension

**Acids, Bases, and Solutions**

# Particles in a Solution (page 225)

***Key Concept:*** **When a solution forms, particles of the solute leave each other and become surrounded by particles of the solvent.**

- Table salt is an ionic solid. When an ionic solid mixes with water, water molecules completely surround the positive ions and the negative ions. The positive ions and negative ions are separated from each other.

- Table sugar is a molecular solid. When a molecular solid mixes with water, the covalent bonds within the sugar molecules are not broken. Sugar breaks up into individual neutral sugar molecules. The individual sugar molecules are completely surrounded by water molecules and are separated from each other.

- A solution of ionic compounds in water can conduct electricity. Separate positive ions and negative ions let electricity flow.

- A solution of molecular compounds in water cannot conduct electricity. Electricity cannot flow when the particles of the solution are all electrically neutral.

*Answer the following questions. Use your textbook and the ideas above.*

5. Circle the letter of each sentence that is true about particles in a solution.

   a. An ionic solid separates into positive ions and negative ions when it dissolves.

   b. A molecular solid separates into neutral molecules when it dissolves.

   c. Table sugar is an ionic solid.

6. Is the following sentence true or false? A solution of ionic compounds in water cannot conduct electricity.

_____

Acids, Bases, and Solutions

# Effects of Solutes on Solvents

(pages 226–227)

***Key Concept:*** **Solutes lower the freezing point and raise the boiling point of a solvent.**

- You can change the freezing point of water by adding solutes to the water. You can also change the boiling point of water by adding solutes to the water.

- Solutes lower the freezing point of a solvent. Pure water freezes at 0°C. A solution of salt water freezes at a colder temperature. The salt particles (solute) make it harder for the water molecules to form crystals.

- Solutes raise the boiling point of a solvent. Pure water boils at 100°C. A solution of salt water boils at a higher temperature. The salt particles (solute) make it harder for water molecules to gain energy and escape into the air as a gas. More energy is needed.

*Answer the following questions. Use your textbook and the ideas above.*

7. Look at the pictures of water particles. Which picture shows liquid water in a saltwater bay? _____

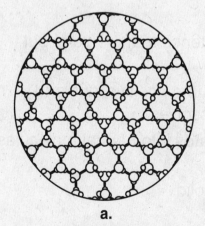
a.

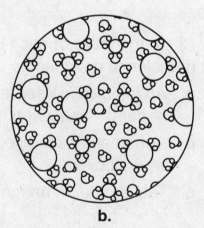
b.

8. Is the following sentence true or false? Water boils at lower temperatures when salt is added to it.

_____

# Concentration and Solubility

**(pages 230–235)**

## Concentration (pages 230–231)

*Key Concept:* **To measure concentration, you compare the amount of solute to the amount of solvent or to the total amount of solution.**

- A **dilute solution** is a mixture that has only a little solute dissolved in a certain amount of solvent. Tree sap is a dilute solution.

- A **concentrated solution** is a mixture that has a lot of solute dissolved in a certain amount of solvent. Maple syrup is a concentrated solution.

- A solution becomes more concentrated if you add solute or take away solvent. A solution becomes more dilute if you add solvent.

- You can describe concentration in a few ways. You can measure the mass of the solute compared to the mass or volume of the solvent. Or you can measure the volume of the solute compared to the volume of the solvent.

*Answer the following questions. Use your textbook and the ideas above.*

1. A mixture that has a lot of solute dissolved in a certain amount of solvent is a(an) _____ solution.

2. A mixture that has only a little solute dissolved in a certain amount of solvent is a(an) _____ solution.

3. Is the following sentence true or false? You can change the concentration of a solution by adding solute.

_____

# Solubility (pages 231–232)

***Key Concept:* Solubility can be used to help identify a substance because it is a characteristic property of matter.**

- **Solubility** describes how much solute can dissolve in a solvent at a given temperature.

- A **saturated solution** is a solution that has so much solute that no more solute will dissolve. A saturated solution is filled up with solute.

- An **unsaturated solution** is a solution that can still dissolve more solute. An unsaturated solution has room to add more solute.

- Solubility tells you how much solute you can dissolve before the solution becomes saturated, or filled up. For example, more sugar than salt will dissolve in 100 g of water. Sugar is more soluble than salt.

- Solubility is a physical property of a substance. You can use solubility to identify an unknown substance.

*Answer the following questions. Use your textbook and the ideas above.*

4. _____ tells how much solute can dissolve in a solvent at a given temperature.

5. A solution that cannot hold any more solute may be described as _____.

**Acids, Bases, and Solutions**

# Factors Affecting Solubility (pages 232–235)

*Key Concept:* **Factors that affect the solubility of a substance include pressure, the type of solvent, and temperature.**

- Pressure affects the solubility of gases. At high pressure, more gas dissolves. Think of opening a soft drink bottle. When you remove the cap, the pressure inside the bottle gets lower and the gas escapes.

- The kind of solvent affects solubility. For example, oil and water do not mix. Oil is a nonpolar compound. Water is a polar compound. Polar compounds and nonpolar compounds do not mix well.

- Temperature affects solubility. At high temperatures, more solid can dissolve. For example, more sugar dissolves in boiling water than in cold water. When the solution cools, the extra sugar stays dissolved. The solution is a **supersaturated solution** because the solution is holding more solute than it normally could. The solution is "super full."

*Answer the following question. Use your textbook and the ideas above.*

6. Complete the concept map about solubility.

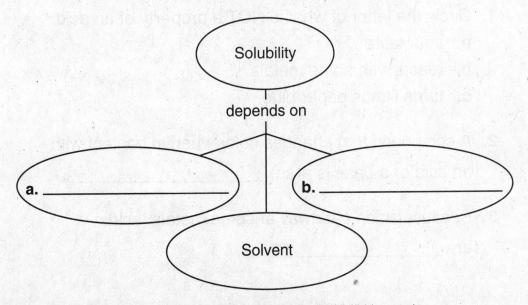

# Describing Acids and Bases

**(pages 236–241)**

## Properties of Acids (pages 236–238)

*Key Concept:* **An acid is a substance that tastes sour, reacts with metals and carbonates, and turns blue litmus paper red.**

- An **acid** is a compound that tastes sour, reacts with metals, and turns blue litmus paper red. Examples of acids are hydrochloric acid and acetic acid.

- Acids tastes sour. Citrus fruits like lemons and grapefruit are acidic. Never taste a chemical to identify it as an acid.

- Acids are corrosive. **Corrosive** means to eat away at other materials. When an acid reacts with some metals, the metals seem to disappear.

- Litmus paper is an indicator. An **indicator** is a compound that changes color when in contact with an acid or a base. Acids turn blue litmus paper red.

*Answer the following questions. Use your textbook and the ideas above.*

1. Circle the letter of what is NOT a property of an acid.
   a. sour taste
   b. reacts with some metals
   c. turns litmus paper blue

2. A compound that changes color when in contact with an acid or a base is a(an) _____.

3. Because acids eat away at some metals, acids are _____.

Acids, Bases, and Solutions

## Properties of Bases (pages 238–239)

*Key Concept:* **A base is a substance that tastes bitter, feels slippery, and turns red litmus paper blue.**

- A **base** is a compound that tastes bitter, feels slippery, and turns litmus paper blue. Bases are the opposite of acids.

- Bases taste bitter. Soaps and detergent taste bitter. Never taste a substance to identify it as a base.

- Bases feel slippery. Soap feels slippery between your fingers. Strong bases can burn your skin. Never touch a substance to identify it as a base.

- Bases turn red litmus paper blue. An easy way to remember this is to remember the letter *b*.

*Answer the following questions. Use your textbook and the ideas above.*

4. Circle the letter of what is NOT a property of a base.
   a. sour taste
   b. slippery feel
   c. turns litmus paper blue

5. Is the following sentence true or false? It is safe to taste or touch an unknown substance to identify it as a base. _____

## Uses of Acids and Bases (pages 240–241)

*Key Concept:* **Acids and bases have many uses around the home and in industry.**

- Acids found in foods like tomatoes and oranges have important jobs in your body.

- Fertilizer and batteries contain acids.

**Acids, Bases, and Solutions**

- Baking soda is a base that makes cakes and cookies light and fluffy.

- Many cleaning products have bases. Cement is made with bases.

*Answer the following questions. Use your textbook and the ideas on page 107 and above.*

**6.** The picture shows two foods, a lemon and a cake. Circle the food that has an acid. Underline the food that is made with a base.

**7.** Draw a line from each type of compound to its use. Compounds can be used more than once.

| Compound | Use |
| --- | --- |
| acid | **a.** fertilizer |
| | **b.** cleaning products |
| base | **c.** cement |
| | **d.** batteries |

# Acids and Bases in Solution (pages 242–247)

## Acids and Bases in Solution (pages 242–243)

***Key Concept:*** **An acid is any substance that produces hydrogen ions (H$^+$) in water. A base is any substance that produces hydroxide ions (OH$^-$) in water.**

- When acids are mixed with water, hydrogen ions and negative ions form. A **hydrogen ion (H$^+$)** is an atom of hydrogen that has lost its electron. This is what happens when hydrochloric acid mixes with water:

$$HCl \rightarrow H^+ + Cl^-$$

- Hydrogen ions are important to the way acids react with other compounds. Hydrogen ions react with blue litmus paper and turn it red.

- The **hydroxide ion (OH$^-$)** is a negative ion made of oxygen and hydrogen. When bases dissolve in water, the positive ions and negative ions separate. This is what happens to sodium hydroxide:

$$NaOH \rightarrow Na^+ + OH^-$$

- Hydroxide ions cause the bitter taste and slippery feel of bases. Hydroxide ions turn red litmus paper blue.

*Answer the following questions. Use your textbook and the ideas above.*

1. A(An) _____ produces hydrogen ions (H$^+$) in water.

2. A(An) _____ produces hydroxide ions (OH$^-$) in water.

**Acids, Bases, and Solutions**

# Strength of Acids and Bases (pages 244–245)

*Key Concept:* **A low pH tells you that the concentration of hydrogen ions is high. In contrast, a high pH tells you that the concentration of hydrogen ions is low.**

- Acids may be strong or weak. A strong acid produces more hydrogen ions when dissolved in water than an equal concentration of weak acid.

- Bases may be strong or weak. A strong base produces more hydroxide ions when dissolved in water than an equal concentration of weak base.

- The **pH scale** is a range of numbers from 0 to 14. The pH tells the concentration of hydrogen ions in a solution. If a solution has a high concentration of hydrogen ions, it is an acid. A pH lower than 7 is acidic.

- If a solution has a low concentration of hydrogen ions, it is a base. A pH higher than 7 is basic.

- A pH equal to 7 means that the solution is neither an acid nor a base. The solution is neutral. Pure water has a pH of 7.

*Answer the following questions. Use your textbook and the ideas above.*

3. Circle the letter of what a strong acid has.

   **a.** many hydroxide ions ($OH^-$)

   **b.** many hydrogen ions ($H^+$)

   **c.** few hydrogen ions ($H^+$)

**Acids, Bases, and Solutions**

4. Look at the pH scale below. Circle the part of the scale where the basic substances are.

pH Scale

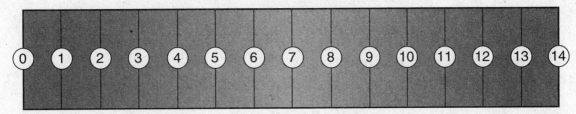

## Acid-Base Reactions (pages 246–247)

***Key Concept:*** In a neutralization reaction, an acid reacts with a base to produce a salt and water.

- A reaction between an acid and a base is called a **neutralization reaction**. An example of a neutralization reaction is:

$$HCl + NaOH \rightarrow H_2O + Na^+ + Cl^-$$

- The reactants in a neutralization reaction are an acid (HCl) and a base (NaOH).

- One product of a neutralization reaction is water. The other product is a salt. A **salt** is any ionic compound made from the positive ion of a base and the negative ion of an acid.

*Answer the following questions. Use your textbook and the ideas above.*

5. A reaction between an acid and a base is called a(an)

   _____ reaction.

6. One product of a neutralization reaction is a(an)

   _____.

Acids, Bases, and Solutions

# Digestion and pH (pages 250–253)

## What Is Digestion? (pages 250–251)

*Key Concept:* Foods must be broken down into simpler substances that your body can use for raw materials and energy.

- Food must be broken down into smaller molecules before your body can use it. In **digestion**, the body breaks down large food molecules into smaller molecules.

- The first part of digestion is a physical change. **Mechanical digestion** is when large food pieces are torn and ground into smaller pieces.

- The second part of digestion is a chemical change. **Chemical digestion** breaks large molecules into smaller molecules in chemical reactions. Some molecules are used as building blocks for the body. Other molecules are used as energy.

- Catalysts in the body help chemical digestion occur. These catalysts are called enzymes. Enzymes must have the right temperature and the right pH to work.

*Answer the following question. Use your textbook and the ideas above.*

1. Draw a line from each term to its meaning.

| Term | Meaning |
|------|---------|
| mechanical digestion | **a.** large food pieces are torn and ground into smaller pieces |
| chemical digestion | **b.** large molecules are broken into smaller molecules in chemical reactions |

**Acids, Bases, and Solutions**

# pH in the Digestive System (pages 252–253)

***Key Concept:*** **Some digestive enzymes work at a low pH. For others, the pH must be high or neutral.**

- Digestion begins in your mouth. Your teeth break food into smaller pieces. Saliva has an enzyme that breaks large sugar molecules into smaller sugar molecules. This enzyme works best at a pH near 7, which is the pH of your mouth.

- The next stage of digestion happens in your stomach. The stomach has a pH of 2. An enzyme in the stomach that breaks large food molecules into small molecules works best at a low pH.

- Digestion finishes in the small intestine. The pH of the small intestine is about 8. In the small intestine, small molecules of food pass into the blood. The blood carries these molecules to the cells that will use them.

*Answer the following questions. Use your textbook and the ideas above.*

**2.** Is the following sentence true or false? Only mechanical digestion takes place in the mouth.

_____

**3.** Look at the picture of the digestive system. Circle the letter of the organ where pH is the lowest.

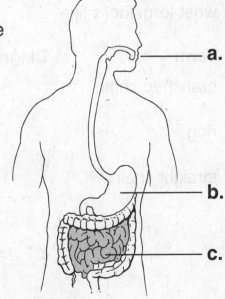

a.

b.

c.

# Properties of Carbon (pages 260–263)

## Carbon Atoms and Bonding (page 261)

*Key Concept:* **Few elements have the ability of carbon to bond with both itself and other elements in so many different ways. With four valence electrons, each carbon atom is able to form four bonds.**

- The atomic number of carbon is 6. An atom of carbon has six protons and six electrons. Four of the electrons are valence electrons. A carbon atom is stable when it has four more valence electrons.

- Carbon is able to form four chemical bonds with other elements and with itself.

- Carbon atoms can form straight chains, branched chains, and rings.

*Answer the following questions. Use your textbook and the ideas above.*

1. How many valence electrons does carbon have?

   **a.** 2          **b.** 4          **c.** 6

2. Draw a line from each term to the diagram that shows what term looks like.

| Term | Diagram |
|------|---------|
| branched chain | **a.** $-\overset{\mid}{\underset{\mid}{C}}-\overset{\mid}{\underset{\mid}{C}}-\overset{\mid}{\underset{\mid}{C}}-$ |
| ring | **b.** $-\overset{\mid}{\underset{\mid}{C}}-\overset{\mid}{\underset{\mid}{C}}-\overset{\mid}{\underset{\mid}{C}}-\overset{\mid}{\underset{\mid}{C}}-$ |
| straight chain | **c.** |

**Carbon Chemistry**

# Forms of Pure Carbon (pages 262–263)

*Key Concept:* **Diamond, graphite, fullerenes, and nanotubes are four forms of the element carbon.**

- Pure carbon is found in different forms. These forms of carbon exist because of the ways that carbon can form chemical bonds.

- **Diamond** is the hardest mineral. Carbon atoms form diamond crystals only at very high temperatures and high pressures.

- **Graphite** is a form of carbon in which each carbon atom is tightly bonded to three other carbon atoms in flat layers. These layers easily slide past each other.

- **Fullerene** is a form of carbon that scientists made. The carbon atoms in a fullerene are arranged in the shape of a hollow sphere.

- A **nanotube** is another form of carbon made by scientists. In a nanotube, carbon atoms are arranged in the shape of a long, hollow tube.

*Answer the following questions. Use your textbook and the ideas above.*

3. Is the following sentence true or false? Pure carbon is found in different forms because of the way it forms bonds. _____

4. Draw a line from each form of carbon to the arrangement of its atoms.

| Form of Carbon | Arrangement of Atoms |
|---|---|
| diamond | **a.** hollow sphere |
| graphite | **b.** crystal |
| fullerene | **c.** flat layers |
| nanotube | **d.** long, hollow tube |

**Carbon Chemistry**

**Carbon Chemistry**

# Carbon Compounds (pages 264–272)

## Organic Compounds (page 265)

*Key Concept:* **Many organic compounds have similar properties in terms of melting points, boiling points, odor, electrical conductivity, and solubility.**

- **Organic compounds** are compounds that contain carbon. Organic compounds are found in all living things. They are also found in products made by living things, such as wood and cotton. Organic compounds are also found in things made by people, such as gasoline and plastics.

- Organic compounds have low melting points and low boiling points. So, many organic compounds are liquids or gases at room temperature.

- Organic liquids often have strong odors.

- Organic compounds do not conduct electricity.

- Organic compounds do not dissolve well in water.

*Answer the following questions. Use your textbook and the ideas above.*

1. Circle the letter of the correct answer. An organic compound is a compound that
   a. is made only by people.
   b. is made only by plants.
   c. contains carbon.

2. Circle the letter of each sentence that is true about organic compounds.
   a. Organic compounds are always solids at room temperature.
   b. Organic compounds conduct electricity.
   c. Organic compounds do not dissolve well in water.

# Hydrocarbons (pages 266–267)

*Key Concept:* **Like many other organic compounds, hydrocarbons mix poorly with water. Also, all hydrocarbons are flammable.**

- A **hydrocarbon** is an organic compound that is made up only of carbon and hydrogen. Methane and propane are hydrocarbons.

- Hydrocarbons do not dissolve well in water.

- Hydrocarbons are flammable. They burn very easily.

- The simplest hydrocarbon is methane. The chemical formula for methane is $CH_4$. The chemical formula shows you that methane has one carbon atom and four hydrogen atoms.

- Propane ($C_3H_8$) has three carbon atoms and eight hydrogen atoms.

*Answer the following questions. Use your textbook and the ideas above.*

3. Read each word in the box. In each sentence below, fill in one of the words.

| | | | |
|---|---|---|---|
| flammable | hydrogen | oxygen | water |

   a. Hydrocarbons are made up of only the elements

   carbon and _____.

   b. Hydrocarbons do not dissolve well in

   _____.

   c. Hydrocarbons burn very easily, which means

   they are _____.

**Carbon Chemistry**

4. Fill in the table below about chemical formulas of hydrocarbons.

| Hydrocarbons | | |
|---|---|---|
| **Chemical Formula** | **Number of Carbon Atoms** | **Number of Hydrogen Atoms** |
| a. _____ | 1 | 4 |
| $C_2H_6$ | b. _____ | 6 |
| $C_3H_8$ | 3 | c. _____ |

# Structure and Bonding in Hydrocarbons (pages 267–269)

*Key Concept:* **The carbon chains in a hydrocarbon may be straight, branched, or ring-shaped. In addition to forming a single bond, two carbon atoms can form a double bond or a triple bond.**

- Chemists use structural formulas to show how atoms in a molecule are arranged. A **structural formula** shows the kind, number, and arrangement of atoms in a molecule.

- In a structural formula, a dash shows a bond (C—C).

- Some molecules can be arranged in different ways. Compounds that have the same chemical formula, but different structures are called **isomers**. Butane ($C_4H_{10}$) has two isomers. One isomer is a straight chain. The other isomer is a branched chain. These isomers of butane have different properties.

**Carbon Chemistry**

- Carbon can also form double bonds and triple bonds. In a structural formula, a double bond is shown by a double dash ($C=C$). A triple bond is shown by a triple dash ($C\equiv C$).

*Answer the following questions. Use your textbook and the ideas on page 118 and above.*

5. In a structural formula, a dash shows a(an)

   _____.

6. This structural formula for propane ($C_3H_8$) is not complete. Complete this structural formula by showing all the hydrogen atoms that are bonded to the carbon chain.

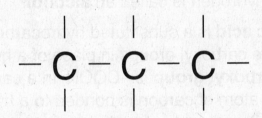

7. Compounds with the same chemical formula but different structures are called _____.

**Carbon Chemistry**

# Substituted Hydrocarbons (pages 270–271)

***Key Concept:*** **If just one atom of another element is substituted for a hydrogen atom in a hydrocarbon, a different compound is created.**

- In a **substituted hydrocarbon**, atoms of other elements replace one or more hydrogen atoms in the hydrocarbon.

- In some substituted hydrocarbons, one or more halogen atoms replace hydrogen atoms. Elements in the halogen family include fluorine, chlorine, bromine, and iodine.

- A **hydroxyl** (hy DRAHKS il) **group** is made up of an oxygen atom and a hydrogen atom (–OH). A substituted hydrocarbon that has one or more hydroxyl groups in place of a hydrogen is called an **alcohol**.

- An **organic acid** is a substituted hydrocarbon that has one or more carboxyl groups in place of a hydrogen atom. A **carboxyl group** is –COOH. In a carboxyl group, one atom of carbon is bonded to a hydroxyl group (–OH) and double bonded to an oxygen atom.

*Answer the following questions. Use your textbook and the ideas above.*

**8.** Read each word in the box. In each sentence below, fill in the correct word or words.

| carboxyl group | halogen | hydroxyl group |
|---|---|---|

    **a.** An atom of oxygen bonded to an atom of hydrogen (–OH) is called a _____.

    **b.** An atom of carbon bonded to an oxygen atom and a hydroxyl group (–COOH) is called a

    _____.

**Carbon Chemistry**

9. Complete the concept map about substituted hydrocarbons.

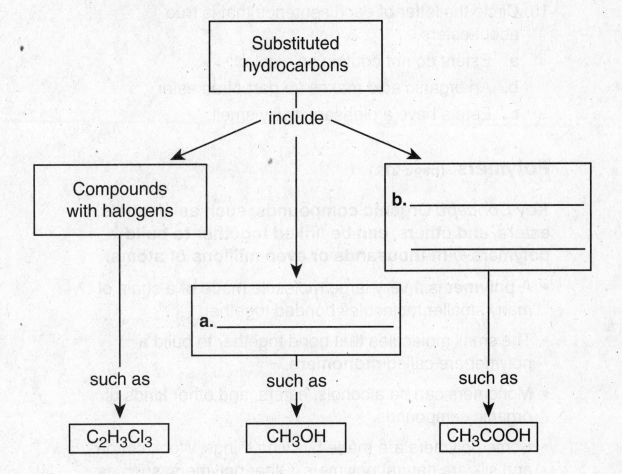

**Esters** (page 271)

*Key Concept:* **Many esters have pleasant, fruity smells.**

- An **ester** is a compound made by chemically combining an alcohol and an organic acid.

- Esters cause the pleasant smell of pineapples, bananas, strawberries, and apples.

**Carbon Chemistry**

*Answer the following question. Use your textbook and the ideas on page 121.*

10. Circle the letter of each sentence that is true about esters.

   **a.** Esters do not contain an alcohol.

   **b.** An organic acid makes up part of an ester.

   **c.** Esters have a pleasant, fruity smell.

# Polymers (page 272)

*Key Concept:* **Organic compounds, such as alcohols, esters, and others, can be linked together to build polymers with thousands or even millions of atoms.**

- A **polymer** is a very large molecule made of a chain of many smaller molecules bonded together.

- The small molecules that bond together to build a polymer are called **monomers**.

- Monomers can be alcohols, esters, and other kinds of organic compounds.

- Some polymers are made by living things. Wool, cotton, and silk are natural polymers. Other polymers, such as nylon and plastic, are made by people.

*Answer the following questions. Use your textbook and the ideas above.*

11. Is the following sentence true or false? A monomer is a very large molecule made of a chain of smaller

   molecules bonded together. _____

12. Circle the letter of a polymer that is made by people.

   **a.** plastic

   **b.** silk

   **c.** wool

**Carbon Chemistry**

# Polymers and Composites
**(pages 274–281)**

## Forming Polymers (page 275)

*Key Concept:* **Polymers form when chemical bonds link large numbers of monomers in a repeating pattern.**

- A polymer (PAHL uh mur) is a large compound built from smaller compounds in a repeating pattern. Plastic is a polymer. Silk is a polymer, too.

- The small compounds that join to form polymers are called monomers (MAHN uh murz). Polymers can be made of one kind of monomer. Polymers can also be made of two or three monomers joined together in a pattern.

- Polymers are often made of compounds that have the element carbon. Carbon can form many compounds. Carbon atoms can form four chemical bonds. Carbon atoms can join to make compounds with straight chains, branched chains, or rings.

*Answer the following questions. Use your textbook and the ideas above.*

1. Read each word in the box. In each sentence below, fill in the correct word or words.

| monomer | polymer | chemical bond |

a. A large compound built from smaller repeating units is a _____.

b. A small compound that joins to form larger compounds is a _____.

**Carbon Chemistry**

2. Look at the carbon compounds below. Circle the letter of the carbon compound that is a ring.

a.                              b.                              c.

# Polymers and Composites (pages 276–280)

*Key Concept:* **Many composite materials include one or more polymers.**

• Many plants and animals make polymers. Plants make a polymer called cellulose (SEL yoo lohs).

• Within your body, **proteins** are polymers formed from smaller molecules called amino acids. An **amino acid** is a monomer that is a building block of proteins.

• Many polymers are made by people. **Plastic** is a polymer made by people that can be molded into different shapes. Carpet and glue are also made of polymers that people have made.

• A **composite** is made of two or more different substances. A composite has different properties than the substances it is made of. Wood is a natural composite. Fiberglass is a composite of glass and plastic.

*Answer the following questions. Use your textbook and the ideas above.*

3. A protein is a polymer formed from monomers called
   **a.** plastics.
   **b.** cellulose.
   **c.** amino acids.

4. Circle the letter of each sentence that is true about composites.

   a. A composite is made from two or more substances.

   b. A composite has the same properties as the substances it is made of.

   c. Wood is a composite.

## Too Many Polymers? (pages 280–281)

**Key Concept: Synthetic polymers are inexpensive to make, strong, and last a long time. As a result, plastics increase the volume of trash.**

- Plastics are very useful and cheap to make. Many things are made of plastic. Some grocery bags are plastic. Milk jugs are plastic, too.

- Many plastics are thrown in the trash. Plastics do not break down into simpler materials in the environment. Plastics may last for many years. As a result, plastics increase the amount of trash.

- One way to reduce the amount of plastic trash is to recycle it. Recycled plastics are used to make bottles, clothing, and park benches.

*Answer the following questions. Use your textbook and the ideas above.*

5. Plastics increase the amount of trash because plastics

   a. break down very quickly into simpler materials.

   b. do not break down into simpler materials in the environment.

   c. do not have very many uses.

6. Is the following sentence true or false? One way to reduce plastic trash is to recycle it. _____

# Life With Carbon (pages 284–291)

## Carbohydrates (pages 285–286)

*Key Concept:* **Carbohydrates are one class of organic compounds required by living things. Starch and cellulose are both polymers built from glucose, but the glucose molecules are arranged differently in each case.**

- A **carbohydrate** is an organic compound made from carbon, hydrogen, and oxygen. Carbohydrates are rich in energy.

- The simplest carbohydrates are sugars. **Glucose** is the most important sugar in your body. The cells in your body use glucose for energy.

- A **complex carbohydrate** is a polymer. Most of the foods you eat are complex carbohydrates.

- **Starch** is a polymer made from glucose. Plants store food in the form of starch. Cereals, rice, and potatoes are foods rich in starch.

- **Cellulose** is another plant polymer made from glucose. Cellulose is part of the stems and roots of plants. Most fruits and vegetables are high in cellulose. Your body, however, cannot break down cellulose to use as energy. Cellulose is an important source of fiber in your diet.

*Answer the following questions. Use your textbook and the ideas above.*

1. Circle the letter of an organic compound that is made of carbon, hydrogen, and oxygen and is rich in energy.
   a. polymer
   b. carbohydrate
   c. isomer

**2.** Complete the concept map about carbohydrates.

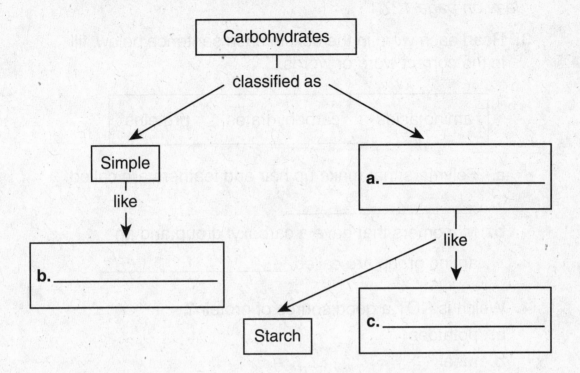

## Proteins (page 287)

*Key Concept:* **Proteins are one class of organic compounds required by living things. Different proteins are made when different sequences of amino acids are linked into long chains.**

- **Proteins** are polymers made of smaller molecules called amino acids. Hair, skin, feathers, and spider webs are all made of protein.

- **Amino acids** are monomers that make up proteins. There are 20 different amino acids. Different combinations of amino acids make different proteins.

- Every amino acid has a carboxyl group (–COOH) and an amino group ($-NH_2$).

- Meat, fish, eggs, and milk are foods that have protein. Your body uses protein to build and repair body parts. Proteins also control the chemical reactions that happen in your body.

*Answer the following questions. Use your textbook and the ideas on page 127.*

**3.** Read each word in the box. In each sentence below, fill in the correct word or words.

| |
|---|
| amino acids    carbohydrates    proteins |

**a.** Polymers that make up hair and feathers are called _____.

**b.** Monomers that have a carboxyl group and an amino group are called _____.

**4.** Which is NOT a good source of protein?
   **a.** potatoes
   **b.** meat
   **c.** milk

# Lipids (pages 288–289)

**Key Concept: Lipids are one class of organic compounds required by living things. Gram for gram, lipids release twice as much energy in your body as do carbohydrates.**

- **Lipids** are made of carbon, hydrogen, and oxygen. Lipids are very rich in energy. Lipids release much more energy in your body than do carbohydrates.

- Fats and oils are lipids. Fats are found in foods like meat and butter. Oils are found in foods like peanuts and olives.

- Fats and oils are both made from three fatty acids and one alcohol called glycerol. A **fatty acid** is a monomer of lipids.

**Carbon Chemistry**

*Answer the following questions. Use your textbook and the ideas on page 128.*

**5.** Is the following sentence true or false? Lipids release much more energy in your body than do

carbohydrates. _____

**6.** Draw a line from each kind of lipid to its food source. Each lipid may be used more than once.

| Lipid | Food Source |
|-------|-------------|
| fat | **a.** meat |
| | **b.** peanuts |
| oil | **c.** butter |
| | **d.** olives |

# Nucleic Acids (pages 289–290)

***Key Concept:*** **Nucleic acids are one class of organic compounds required by living things. The differences among living things depend on the order of nucleotides in their DNA.**

- **Nucleic** (noo KLAY ik) **acids** are very large organic molecules made up of carbon, oxygen, hydrogen, nitrogen, and phosphorus. One kind of nucleic acid is **DNA**, or deoxyribonucleic (dee AHK see ry boh noo klay ik) acid.

- **Nucleotides** (NOO klee oh tydz) are the monomers that join together to make nucleic acids. Only four different nucleotides make up a molecule of DNA.

- The order of nucleotides in a DNA molecule determines the order of amino acids in a protein.

**Carbon Chemistry**

- Different DNA molecules produce different proteins, which cause living things to differ from each other.

- When living things reproduce, they pass DNA molecules to their offspring.

*Answer the following questions. Use your textbook and the ideas on page 129 and above.*

**7.** The pictures show two different organic compounds. Circle the letter of the nucleic acid.

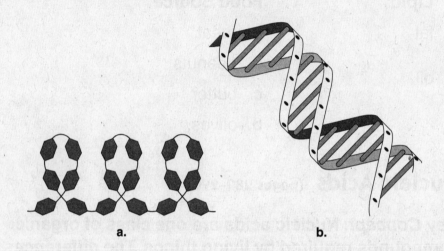

a.                                        b.

**8.** Circle the letter of each sentence that is true about nucleic acids.

   **a.** Nucleic acids are made up of amino acids.

   **b.** The order of nucleotides in a DNA molecule determines the order of amino acids in a protein.

   **c.** Living things pass on DNA molecules to their offspring.

**Carbon Chemistry**

# Other Compounds in Foods (pages 290–291)

*Key Concept:* **Unlike carbohydrates, proteins, and lipids, your body needs vitamins and minerals in only small amounts.**

- Vitamins are organic compounds. Vitamins are molecules that help chemical reactions take place in your body. For example, vitamin C helps keep your skin and gums healthy.

- Minerals are elements in the form of ions. Minerals are not organic compounds. Minerals are important in many different body process. Some minerals you need are calcium and iron.

- Water ($H_2O$) is not an organic compound. Your body must have water to survive. Water makes up most of the liquids in your body. Water in the blood helps carry nutrients to body cells. Water also carries wastes away from cells.

*Answer the following questions. Use your textbook and the ideas above.*

**9.** Is the following sentence true or false? Your body needs vitamins and minerals in only small amounts.

_____

**10.** Draw a line from each term to its meaning.

| Term | Meaning |
|------|---------|
| vitamins | **a.** elements in the form of ions that help in body processes |
| minerals | **b.** a compound that makes up most body liquids |
| water | **c.** organic compounds that help chemical reactions take place in the body |

**Motion**

# Describing and Measuring
# Motion (pages 308–311)

## Describing Motion (pages 309–310)

*Key Concept:* **An object is in motion if it changes position relative to a reference point.**

- **Motion** means moving. To find out if an object is in motion, you must compare it to another object or place. An object is in motion if its distance from another object or place is changing.

- A **reference point** is an object or place that you can use to tell if an object is in motion. A tree, a sign, or a building make good reference points.

- Whether or not an object is in motion depends on the reference point. Suppose you are sitting in a chair. If your chair is your reference point, you are not moving. But if you choose the sun as your reference point, you are moving quite fast. This is because you and your chair are on Earth, which moves around the sun.

*Answer the following questions. Use your textbook and the ideas above.*

1. Read each word in the box. In each sentence below, fill in the correct word or words.

| reference point | force | motion |
|---|---|---|

   **a.** An object is in _____ if its distance from another object or place is changing.

   **b.** To see if an object is moving, you must compare it to a _____.

**Motion**

2. Is the following sentence true or false? Whether or not an object is in motion depends on the reference point.

_____

# Measuring Distance (pages 310–311)

*Key Concept:* **Scientists use SI units to describe the distance an object moves.**

- The system of measurement that scientists all over the world use is called the **International System of Units**. The abbreviation for the system of units is SI.

- The SI unit of length is the meter (m). A meter is a little longer than a yard.

- The length of an object smaller than a meter often is measured in a unit called the centimeter (cm). There are 100 centimeters in a meter.

- Distances too long to be measured in meters often are measured in kilometers. There are 1,000 meters in a kilometer.

- Scientists also use SI units to measure quantities other than length.

*Answer the following questions. Use your textbook and the ideas above.*

3. When you are measuring in an SI unit, you are using

the _____ System of Units.

4. Circle the letter of the SI unit of length.
   a. centimeter
   b. meter
   c. kilometer

5. Is the following sentence true or false? There are 1,000

meters in a centimeter. _____

**Motion**

# Speed and Velocity (pages 312–317)

## Calculating Speed (pages 312–313)

*Key Concept:* **If you know the distance an object travels in a certain amount of time, you can calculate the speed of the object.**

- **Speed** is a rate. It tells how far something moves in a certain amount of time. For example, *1 meter per second* is a speed.

- To find speed, use the formula:

$$\text{Speed} = \frac{\text{Distance}}{\text{Time}}$$

- On a bike ride, you slow down and speed up. **Average speed** tells the total distance you rode divided by the total time it took. **Instantaneous speed** is the speed you were moving at an instant in time during the bike ride.

*Answer the following questions. Use your textbook and the ideas above.*

1. Read the words in the box. Use the correct words to fill in the blanks in the formula for speed.

   | Distance | Rate | Time |
   | --- | --- | --- |

   $$\text{Speed} = \frac{\text{a. } \underline{\hspace{4cm}}}{\text{b. } \underline{\hspace{4cm}}}$$

2. Is the following sentence true or false? Your average speed on a bike ride was the speed you were moving at an instant in time during the ride. _____

**Motion**

3. How would you find the speed of a person who walked 10 meters in 8 seconds? Circle the letter of the correct answer.
    a. Speed = 10 meters ÷ 8 seconds
    b. Speed = 8 seconds × 10 meters
    c. Speed = 8 seconds ÷ 10 meters

## Describing Velocity (pages 314–315)

*Key Concept:* **When you know both the speed and direction of an object's motion, you know the velocity of the object.**

- **Velocity** is speed in a given direction.

- For example, the velocity of a person walking is 3 kilometers per hour, west. This tells the speed the person is walking. It also tells you the direction the person is walking.

*Answer the following questions. Use your textbook and the ideas above.*

4. Speed in a given direction is _____.

5. What do you need to know to describe the velocity of an object? Circle the letter of each thing you need to know.
    a. distance
    b. direction
    c. speed

6. A velocity tells speed and direction. Circle the letter of each velocity.
    a. 2 meters per second east
    b. 5 kilometers per hour
    c. 10 meters per second west

## Graphing Motion (pages 316–317)

***Key Concept:*** **You can show the motion of an object on a line graph in which you plot distance versus time.**

- Motion can be shown on a line graph. A motion graph shows time along the bottom, or *x*-axis. A motion graph shows distance along the side, or *y*-axis.

- The steepness of the line on the graph is called **slope**. A line that rises steeply shows that an object is moving quickly. A line that rises less steeply shows that an object is moving more slowly. A line that is flat shows that an object is not moving at all.

*Answer the following questions. Use your textbook and the ideas above.*

7. The steepness of the line on a graph is called

   _____.

8. Look at the graph. Which part of the line shows a time when the object was not moving?
   a. A
   b. B
   c. C

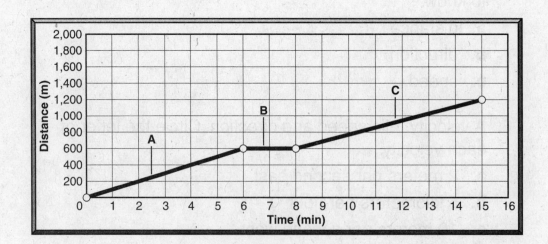

**Motion**

# Acceleration (pages 320–325)

## What Is Acceleration? (pages 320–321)

*Key Concept:* In science, acceleration refers to increasing speed, decreasing speed, or changing direction.

- Remember that velocity is speed and direction. **Acceleration** is the rate at which velocity changes.

- Objects accelerate when they speed up. A car that goes faster is accelerating.

- Objects accelerate when they slow down. A rolling ball that slows down is accelerating.

- Objects accelerate when they change direction. A bus that turns a corner is accelerating.

*Answer the following questions. Use your textbook and the ideas above.*

1. The rate at which velocity changes is

   _____.

2. Circle the letter of each example of acceleration.
   a. A ball speeds up as it rolls down a hill.
   b. A car slows down as it comes to a stop sign.
   c. A biker goes around a curved track without changing speed.

3. Is the following sentence true or false? A bus stopped at a red light is accelerating. _____

**Motion**

# Calculating Acceleration (pages 322–323)

***Key Concept:*** **To determine the acceleration of an object moving in a straight line, you must calculate the change in speed per unit of time.**

- You can find the acceleration of an object moving in a straight line.

- To find acceleration, you need to know three things:
  1. You need to know the starting speed.
  2. You need to know the ending speed.
  3. You need to know how long it took for the object to change speeds.

- The formula for acceleration is:

$$\text{Acceleration} = \frac{\text{Final speed} - \text{Initial speed}}{\text{Time}}$$

- The unit for acceleration is meters per second per second, or $m/s^2$.

*Answer the following questions. Use your textbook and the ideas above.*

4. Read the words in the box. Use the words to fill in the blanks in the formula for acceleration.

| Final speed | Time | Distance |

$$\text{Acceleration} = \frac{\text{a.} _____ - \text{Initial speed}}{\text{b.} _____}$$

5. Is the following sentence true or false? Acceleration is measured in meters per second per second.

_____

**Motion**

6. A student used this formula to find the acceleration of an object:

$$\frac{8 \text{ m/s} - 2 \text{ m/s}}{3 \text{ s}} =$$

a. What is the final speed of the object?

_____

b. What is the initial speed of the object?

_____

c. How long did it take the object to change speeds? _____

## Graphing Acceleration (pages 324–325)

***Key Concept:* You can use both a speed-versus-time graph and a distance-versus-time graph to analyze the motion of an accelerating object.**

- Acceleration can be shown on a line graph.

- A speed-versus-time graph shows time on the bottom, or *x*-axis. It shows speed on the side, or *y*-axis. A straight, slanted line on this kind of graph shows acceleration.

- A distance-versus-time graph shows time on the *x*-axis. It shows distance on the *y*-axis. A curved line on this kind of graph shows acceleration.

*Answer the following questions. Use your textbook and the ideas above.*

7. Circle the letter of the kind of graph that can be used to show acceleration.
   a. circle graph
   b. bar graph
   c. line graph

8. Fill in blanks in the table about acceleration graphs.

| Acceleration Graphs | |
|---|---|
| **Type of Graph** | **Acceleration Is Shown as** |
| a. _____ | straight, slanted line |
| b. _____ | curved line |

9. Use the graphs to answer the questions.

**Graph A**

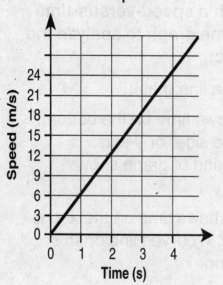

**Graph B**

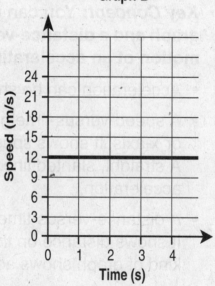

a. Which graph shows an object that is moving at a steady speed? _____

b. Which graph shows an object with a changing speed? _____

c. Which graph shows acceleration?

_____

**Forces**

# The Nature of Force (pages 334–337)

## What Is a Force? (pages 334–335)

*Key Concept:* **Like velocity and acceleration, a force is described by its strength and by the direction in which it acts.**

- A **force** is a push or a pull.

- To tell about a force, you must tell how strong the force is. The SI unit for the strength of a force is the **newton**.

- To tell about a force you must also tell the direction the force is pushing or pulling.

- Arrows can be used to show forces. The point of the arrow shows the direction of the force. The length of the arrow shows how strong the force is.

*Answer the following questions. Use your textbook and the ideas above.*

1. Circle the letter of the arrow that shows the stronger force.

   **a.**                                        **b.**

2. Is the following sentence true or false? Forces are described by their strength and their direction. _____

3. The SI unit used for measuring the strength of a force is the _____.

**4.** Read the words in the box. Use the words to fill in the concept map about force.

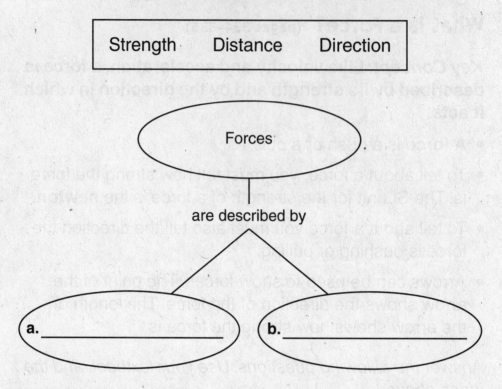

Strength    Distance    Direction

Forces

are described by

a. _____    b. _____

## Combining Forces (pages 335–337)

*Key Concept:* **Unbalanced forces acting on an object result in a net force and cause a change in the object's motion. Balanced forces acting on an object do not change the object's motion.**

- Often there is more than one force acting on an object. The total of all the forces acting on an object is called the **net force**.

- Sometimes the net force on an object is 0. This means there are **balanced forces** acting on the object. The object's motion does not change.

- Sometimes the net force does not equal 0. This means there are **unbalanced forces** acting on the object. The object's motion changes.

**Forces**

*Answer the following questions. Use your textbook and the ideas on page 142.*

**5.** Draw a line from each term to its meaning.

| Term | Meaning |
|------|---------|
| net force | **a.** cause a net force of 0 |
| balanced forces | **b.** the total of the forces acting on an object |
| unbalanced forces | **c.** cause an object's motion to change |

**6.** Label the circles in the Venn diagram to show which circle describes balanced forces and which circle describes unbalanced forces.

**a.** _____     **b.** _____

_____     _____

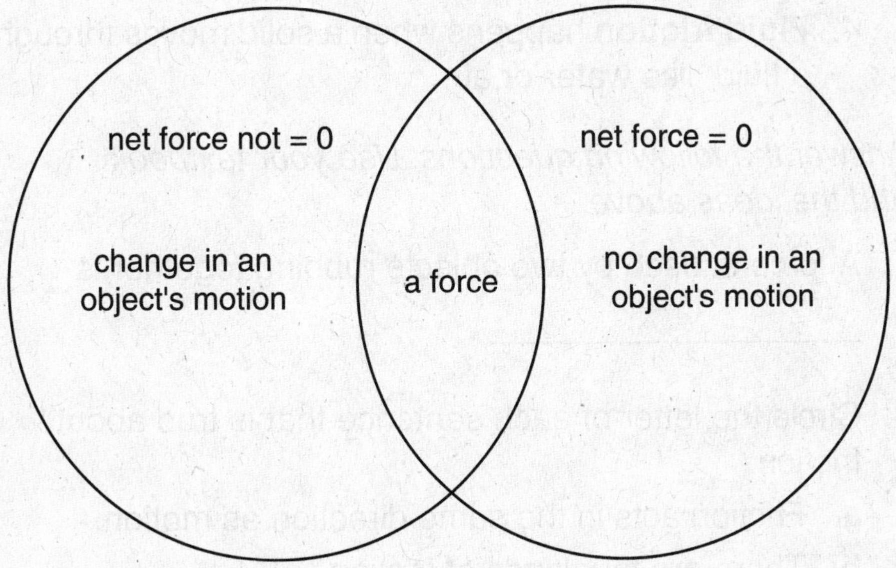

net force not = 0

net force = 0

change in an object's motion

a force

no change in an object's motion

**Forces**

# Friction and Gravity (pages 340–348)

## Friction (pages 341–343)

*Key Concept:* **The strength of the force of friction depends on two factors: how hard the surfaces push together and the types of surfaces involved.**

- **Friction** is a force caused by two objects rubbing together. Friction acts in the opposite direction of motion. Friction keeps you from slipping when you walk. Friction also makes a car's brakes work.

- The amount of friction depends on two things: how smooth the objects are and how hard they push together.

- There are four kinds of friction:
    1. **Static friction** is between two things that are not moving.
    2. **Sliding friction** happens when two objects slide past each other.
    3. **Rolling friction** occurs when one object rolls over another.
    4. **Fluid friction** happens when a solid moves through a fluid, like water or air.

*Answer the following questions. Use your textbook and the ideas above.*

1. A force caused by two objects rubbing together is

   _____.

2. Circle the letter of each sentence that is true about friction.

   a. Friction acts in the same direction as motion.

   b. There are four kinds of friction.

   c. The amount of friction depends only on how smooth the objects are.

**Forces**

3. Friction acts in the opposite direction of

   _____.

4. Read the words in the box. Use the words to fill in the blanks in the table about friction.

| Static friction | Fluid friction | Sliding friction |

| **Friction** | |
| --- | --- |
| **Kind of Friction** | **Friction Occurs When...** |
| Rolling friction | an object rolls over a surface |
| a. _____ _____ | an object moves through air or water |
| b. _____ _____ | one object slides over another |
| c. _____ _____ | objects are not moving |

**Forces**

# Gravity (pages 344–345)

***Key Concept:*** **Two factors affect the gravitational attraction between objects: mass and distance.**

- **Gravity** is a force that pulls objects toward each other.

- Gravity depends on mass. **Mass** is how much matter is in an object. Objects with a large mass have a greater force of gravity than objects with a small mass.

- Gravity depends on distance. As the distance between objects increases, the force of gravity decreases.

- **Weight** measures the force of gravity on an object. An object's weight can change if the force of gravity changes. An object's mass stays the same no matter where it is.

*Answer the following questions. Use your textbook and the ideas above.*

5. A force that pulls objects toward each other is

   _____.

6. Read each word in the box. In each sentence below, fill in the correct word or words.

   | increases    decreases    stays the same |
   | --- |

   a. If two objects move farther apart, the force of gravity between them _____.

   b. An object's mass _____ if less gravity acts on the object.

7. What is weight? Circle the letter of the correct answer.
   a. a force that pulls objects toward each other
   b. the amount of matter in an object
   c. the force of gravity on an object

Name _____ Date _____ Class _____

**Forces**

# Gravity and Motion (pages 346–348)

***Key Concept:*** **In free fall, the force of gravity is an unbalanced force that causes an object to accelerate.**

- Gravity is the force that pulls objects toward Earth.

- If gravity is the only force pulling on a falling object, the object is in **free fall**.

- Most objects move through air. Friction caused by air is called **air resistance**. Air resistance is a force that pushes upward on falling objects.

- As an object falls to Earth, its velocity increases. The greatest velocity it reaches is called its **terminal velocity**.

*Answer the following question. Use your textbook and the ideas above.*

**8.** Read the words in the box. Use the correct words to label the forces in the picture.

| Gravity | Terminal velocity | Air resistance |
|---------|-------------------|----------------|

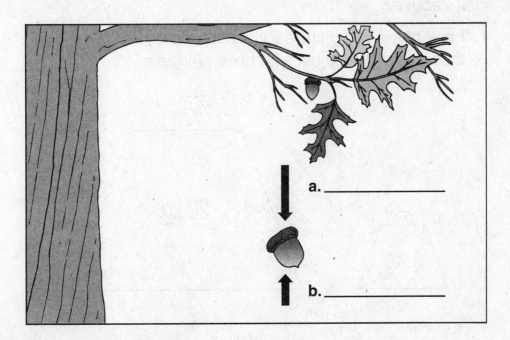

a. _____

b. _____

# Newton's First and Second Laws (pages 349–352)

## The First Law of Motion (pages 349–350)

*Key Concept:* Isaac Newton's first law of motion states that an object at rest will remain at rest, and an object moving at a constant velocity will continue moving at a constant velocity, unless it is acted upon by an unbalanced force.

• Isaac Newton studied motion in the 1600s.

• Newton's first law of motion says that a moving object will not speed up, slow down, or stop unless it is acted on by an unbalanced force. It also says that an object that is not moving will not start moving unless it is acted on by an unbalanced force.

• Objects resist a change in motion. This is called **inertia** (in UR shuh). All objects have inertia. The more mass an object has, the more inertia it has.

*Answer the following questions. Use your textbook and the ideas above.*

1. Look at the two pictures. Circle the letter of the picture that shows the object with greater inertia.

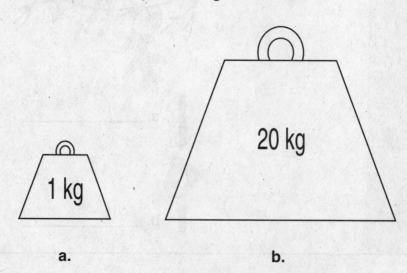

a.                    b.

**Forces**

2. Read the words in the box. Use the correct words to fill in the blanks in the concept map about Newton's first law.

| A moving object | Inertia | An unbalanced force |
| --- | --- | --- |

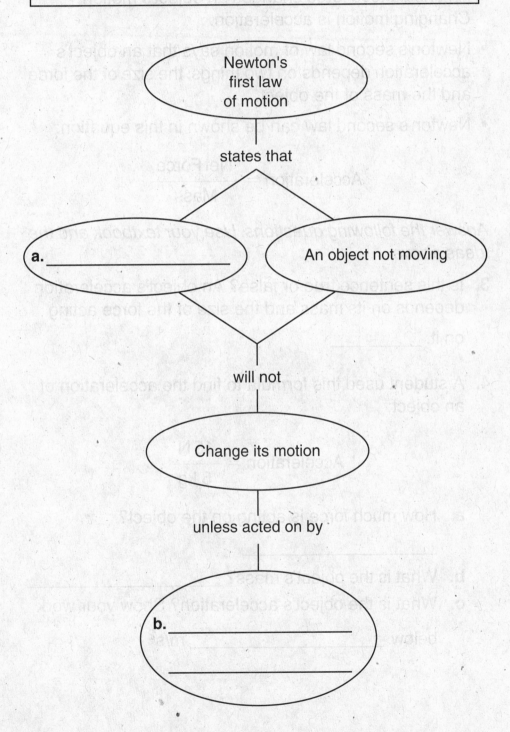

Newton's
first law
of motion

states that

a. _____

An object not moving

will not

Change its motion

unless acted on by

b. _____
_____

**Forces**

# The Second Law of Motion (pages 350–352)

***Key Concept:*** **According to Newton's second law of motion, acceleration depends on the object's mass and on the net force acting on the object.**

- An unbalanced force changes an object's motion. Changing motion is acceleration.

- Newton's second law of motion says that an object's acceleration depends on two things: the size of the force and the mass of the object.

- Newton's second law can be shown in this equation:

$$\text{Acceleration} = \frac{\text{Net Force}}{\text{Mass}}$$

*Answer the following questions. Use your textbook and the ideas above.*

3. Is this sentence true or false? An object's acceleration depends on its mass and the size of the force acting on it. _____

4. A student used this formula to find the acceleration of an object:

$$\text{Acceleration} = \frac{15\,\text{N}}{5\,\text{kg}}$$

   **a.** How much force is acting on the object?

   _____

   **b.** What is the object's mass? _____

   **c.** What is the object's acceleration? Show your work below. _____ $\text{m/s}^2$

**Forces**

# Newton's Third Law (pages 353–359)

## Newton's Third Law of Motion (pages 353–355)

**Key Concept:** Newton's third law of motion states that if one object exerts a force on another object, then the second object exerts a force of equal strength in the opposite direction on the first object.

- Newton's third law of motion says that forces come in pairs. When one object exerts a force on a second object, the second object exerts a force back on the first object. The forces are of equal strength. The forces are opposite in direction.

- These two forces are called action force and reaction force. When you jump, the action force is your legs pushing down on the ground. The reaction force is the ground pushing back on your legs.

*Answer the following question. Use your textbook and the ideas above.*

1. Read the words in the box. Use the words to fill in the blanks in the concept map about action and reaction forces.

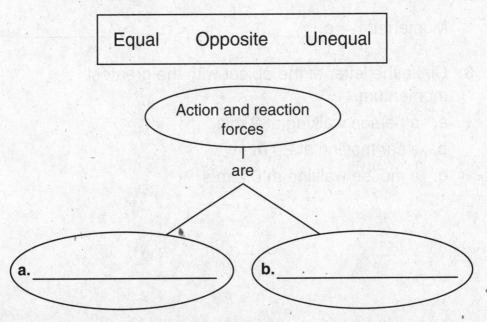

| Equal | Opposite | Unequal |

Action and reaction forces

are

a. _____

b. _____

**Forces**

## Momentum (pages 356–357)

***Key Concept:*** **The momentum of a moving object can be determined by multiplying the object's mass and velocity.**

- The **momentum** (moh MEN tum) of a moving object is its mass times its velocity.

- Momentum has an amount and a direction. The unit for momentum is kg·m/s.

- An object with a large mass or a fast velocity has a large amount of momentum. The more momentum an object has, the harder it is to stop.

- A speeding truck has a large amount of momentum. A small car moving at the same velocity has less momentum than the truck.

*Answer the following questions. Use your textbook and the ideas above.*

2. Read the words in the box. Use the words to fill in the blanks in the formula for momentum.

   | Mass | Velocity | Acceleration |
   |---|---|---|

   Momentum = **a.** _____ × **b.** _____

3. Circle the letter of the object with the greatest momentum.
   - **a.** a person walking at 2 m/s
   - **b.** a car moving at 20 m/s
   - **c.** a mouse walking at 0.2 m/s

**Forces**

# Conservation of Momentum (pages 357–359)

*Key Concept:* **The total momentum of any group of objects remains the same, or is conserved, unless outside forces act on the objects.**

- Moving objects sometimes bump one another. When that happens, some momentum can move from one object to another. However, the total momentum stays the same. This is the law of **conservation of momentum**.

- When one moving object hits an object that is moving at a different velocity, some momentum is passed on, or transferred.

- When a moving object hits an object that is not moving, all of the momentum is transferred to the object that was not moving.

*Answer the following questions. Use your textbook and the ideas above.*

4. Look at the picture. What is the total momentum of the two train cars *after* they collide? _____

**Before**   4 m/s ⟶                          0 m/s

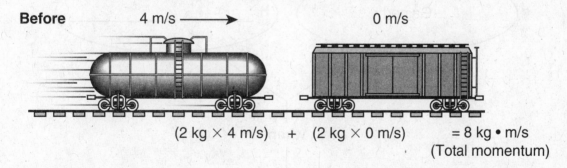

(2 kg × 4 m/s)   +   (2 kg × 0 m/s)        = 8 kg • m/s
                                              (Total momentum)

**After**   0 m/s                            4 m/s ⟶

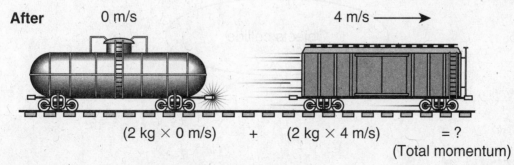

(2 kg × 0 m/s)   +   (2 kg × 4 m/s)        = ?
                                              (Total momentum)

**Forces**

5. Read the words in the box. Use the correct words to fill in the blanks in the concept map about the conservation of momentum.

| Momentum | Velocity | Lost |
|---|---|---|

The
Law of Conservation
of Momentum

says that

a. _____

is not

Gained        or        b. _____

when

Objects collide

# Rockets and Satellites (pages 362–365)

## How Do Rockets Lift Off? (page 363)

*Key Concept:* **A rocket can rise into the air because the gases it expels with a downward action force exert an equal but opposite reaction force on the rocket.**

- Newton's third law of motion explains how rockets and space shuttles lift off.

- When a rocket lifts off, it burns fuel. The gases that come out of the bottom of the rocket push down on Earth. This is the action force.

- The reaction force is the gases pushing back on the rocket. The reaction force pushes upward.

*Answer the following questions. Use your textbook and the ideas above.*

1. Newton's _____ law of motion explains how rockets and space shuttles lift off.

2. Read each word in the box. In each sentence below, fill in one of the words.

| up    down    thrust |
|---|

a. When a rocket lifts off, the action force pushes _____.

b. When a rocket lifts off, the reaction force pushes _____.

3. Read the words in the box. Use the words to label the picture of the space shuttle lifting off.

```
┌─────────────────────────────────────────────┐
│                                               │
│   Action force       Reaction force           │
│                                               │
└─────────────────────────────────────────────┘
```

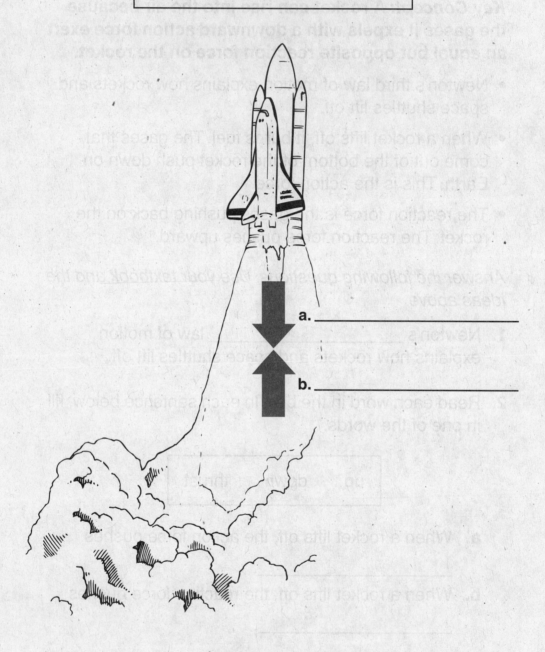

a. _____

b. _____

**Forces**

# What Is a Satellite? (pages 363–365)

***Key Concept:*** **Satellites in orbit around Earth continuously fall toward Earth, but because Earth is curved they travel around it.**

- A **satellite** orbits, or moves around, another object in space.

- Some satellites orbit Earth. These satellites are used for many things. For example, some satellites collect weather data from around the world.

- A force that keeps a satellite in orbit is **centripetal** (sen TRIP ih tul) **force**. The centripetal force pulls the satellite toward the center of the Earth.

*Answer the following questions. Use your textbook and the ideas above.*

4. Read the words in the box. Use the words to label the diagram.

| Earth     Satellite     Centripetal force |
| --- |

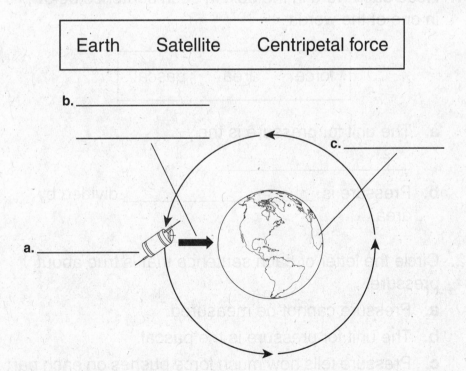

b. _____

_____

c. _____

a. _____

5. The force that keeps a satellite in orbit is

_____.

**Forces in Fluids**

# Pressure (pages 372–378)

## What Is Pressure? (pages 372–373)

*Key Concept:* **Pressure decreases as the area over which a force is distributed increases.**

- **Pressure** tells how much force pushes on each part of a surface.

- The formula for pressure is:

$$\text{Pressure} = \frac{\text{Force}}{\text{Area}}$$

- The unit for pressure is the **pascal** (Pa).

*Answer the following questions. Use your textbook and the ideas above.*

1. Read each word in the box. In each sentence below, fill in one of the words.

   | force | area | pascal |
   |-------|------|--------|

   a. The unit for pressure is the

      _____.

   b. Pressure is _____ divided by area.

2. Circle the letter of each sentence that is true about pressure.

   a. Pressure cannot be measured.

   b. The unit for pressure is the pascal.

   c. Pressure tells how much force pushes on each part of a surface.

## Fluid Pressure (pages 374–375)

**Key Concept: All of the forces exerted by the individual particles in a fluid combine to make up the pressure exerted by the fluid.**

- A **fluid** is a gas, such as air, or a liquid, such as water.

- The tiny particles in a fluid move all the time. They push on everything around them. Fluid pressure is the force exerted by the particles of a fluid.

- Air is a fluid. Air pushes down on everything on Earth. Air pressure is one kind of fluid pressure.

*Answer the following questions. Use your textbook and the ideas above.*

3. Read each word in the box. In each sentence below, fill in one of the words.

| fluid | particles | air pressure |
|---|---|---|

 a. A liquid or a gas is a(an) _____.
 b. All liquids and gases are made up of

 _____.

4. The force exerted by the particles of a fluid is called

 _____.

5. Is the following sentence true or false? Air pressure is

 one kind of fluid pressure. _____

# Variations in Fluid Pressure (pages 376–378)

***Key Concept:*** **As your elevation increases, atmospheric pressure decreases. Water pressure increases as depth increases.**

- There are different amounts of air pressure in different places. There is less air pressure in high places, such as on a mountain top. There is more air pressure in lower places, such as in a valley.

- Water also exerts fluid pressure. The deeper you go in the water, the more water pressure pushes on you.

- Air pressure is measured with a **barometer**.

*Answer the following questions. Use your textbook and the ideas above.*

*Use the picture to answer questions 6 and 7.*

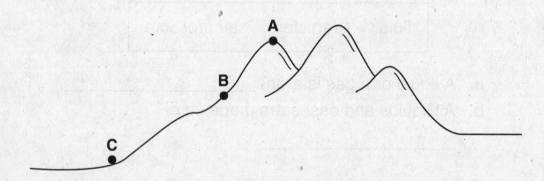

6. At which place is pressure the greatest? _____

7. At which place is there the least pressure? _____

8. Circle the letter of the tool that is used to measure air pressure.
   a. thermometer
   b. barometer
   c. graduated cylinder

Forces in Fluids

# Floating and Sinking (pages 380–385)

## Buoyancy (pages 381–382)

*Key Concept:* The buoyant force acts in the direction opposite to the force of gravity, so it makes an object feel lighter.

- Water and other fluids push up on objects. This upward push is called the **buoyant force**. It makes objects in fluid feel lighter.

- If an object's weight is more than the buoyant force, the object will sink. If an object's weight is equal to the buoyant force, the object will float.

- When an object is placed in a fluid, it takes up space. Some of the fluid needs to move to make room for the object. The weight of the fluid that needs to move is equal to the buoyant force.

- A big object takes up more room than a small object. So a big object is acted on by a greater buoyant force than a small object.

*Answer the following questions. Use your textbook and the ideas above.*

1. The upward push of a fluid on an object is called the

   _____.

2. Circle the letter of each sentence that is true about buoyant force.
   a. It pushes upward.
   b. It makes objects feel lighter.
   c. It pushes downward.

**Forces in Fluids**

**3.** Read each word in the box. Use the words to fill in the blanks in the table about buoyancy.

| sinks | floats |

| Buoyancy | |
|---|---|
| **Object's Weight** | **What the Object Does** |
| More than the buoyant force | a. _____ |
| Equal to the buoyant force | b. _____ |

**4.** Circle the letter of what the buoyant force on an object is equal to.

a. the weight of the object

b. the weight of the fluid the object moves

c. the weight of the air pressing on the object

**Forces in Fluids**

## Density (pages 383–385)

***Key Concept:*** **By comparing densities, you can predict whether an object will sink or float in a fluid.**

- **Density** tells how much mass an object has for its volume. Cork does not have much mass for its volume. Cork has a low density. Lead has more mass for its volume. Lead has a greater density than cork.

- To find density, you can use the formula:

$$\text{Density} = \frac{\text{Mass}}{\text{Volume}}$$

- If an object is more dense than a fluid, the object will sink in that fluid. If an object is less dense than a fluid, the object will float on that fluid.

*Answer the following questions. Use your textbook and the ideas above.*

5. Circle the letter of the formula for density.
   a. Density = Mass + Volume
   b. Density = Mass × Volume
   c. Density = Mass ÷ Volume

6. Fill in the blanks in the table about density.

| Density | |
|---|---|
| **Object's Density** | **What Object Does** |
| More dense than fluid | a. _____ |
| Less dense than fluid | b. _____ |

**Forces in Fluids**

7. The pictures show two objects in water. Both objects have the same volume. Write the letter of the correct sentence under each picture.

   **a.** Object is more dense than water.

   **b.** Object is less dense than water.

   **c.** Object has a density equal to water's density.

_____

**Forces in Fluids**

# Pascal's Principle (pages 388–392)

## Transmitting Pressure in a Fluid
(pages 389–390)

*Key Concept:* **When force is applied to a confined fluid, the change in pressure is transmitted equally to all parts of the fluid.**

- A fluid pushes against its container. This is called fluid pressure. When a container of fluid is squeezed, the fluid pressure increases.

- **Pascal's principle** says that when force is applied to a fluid in a closed container, pressure increases all through the fluid.

- You can see Pascal's principle with a water balloon. When you push in on one part of the balloon, other parts of the balloon bulge out.

- A hydraulic device contains fluid. Force is applied to one part of the device. The change in fluid pressure can be used to multiply the force.

*Answer the following questions. Use your textbook and the ideas above.*

1. Read each word in the box. In each sentence below, fill in the correct word or words.

| fluid | Pascal's principle | pressure |
|---|---|---|

   a. The particles in a _____ push against their container.

   b. According to _____, pressure increases all through a fluid when a force is applied.

**Forces in Fluids**

2. Read the words in the box. Use the words to fill in the concept map about Pascal's principle.

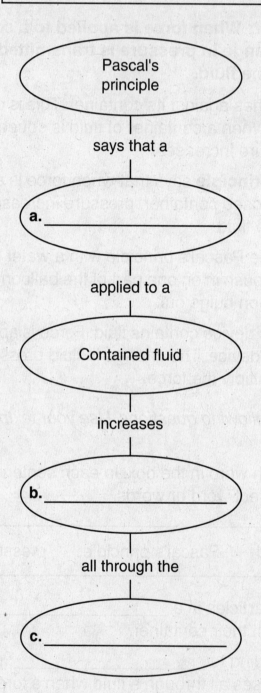

| Pressure | Force | Fluid |

Pascal's principle

says that a

a. _____

applied to a

Contained fluid

increases

b. _____

all through the

c. _____

**Forces in Fluids**

# Hydraulic Systems (pages 391–392)

*Key Concept:* **A hydraulic system multiplies force by applying the force to a small surface area. The increase in pressure is then transmitted to another part of the confined fluid, which pushes on a larger surface area.**

- Hydraulic systems use fluids to transmit pressure. Hydraulic systems multiply force.

- When a hydraulic system is used, a force is applied to a small area. The pressure is transmitted through the fluid. The fluid pushes on a larger area. The pressure stays the same, but the force is multiplied.

- The lifts used in car repair shops use hydraulic systems. So do the chairs at barber shops and beauty salons.

*Answer the following questions. Use your textbook and the ideas above.*

3. Circle the letter of each sentence that is true about hydraulic systems.
   a. Hydraulic systems multiply force.
   b. Hydraulic systems have no uses.
   c. Hydraulic systems contain a fluid.

4. Is the following sentence true or false? In a hydraulic system, pressure is transmitted through a fluid.

   _____

# Bernoulli's Principle

**(pages 393–397)**

## Pressure and Moving Fluids (page 394)

*Key Concept:* Bernoulli's principle states that as the speed of a moving fluid increases, the pressure within the fluid decreases.

- **Bernoulli's principle** says that the faster a fluid moves, the less pressure it exerts.

- Fluid moves from places with high pressure to places with low pressure. When you suck on a drinking straw, you make an area of low pressure in the straw. This causes the fluid in the cup to move up the straw.

*Answer the following questions. Use your textbook and the ideas above.*

1. Is the following sentence true or false? The faster a fluid moves, the more pressure it exerts. _____

2. Circle the letter of what happens when a fluid moves faster.
   a. It exerts more pressure.
   b. The pressure it exerts does not change.
   c. It exerts less pressure.

3. Fluids move from places of high pressure to places with _____ pressure.

**Forces in Fluids**

# Applying Bernoulli's Principle (pages 395–397)

***Key Concept:*** Bernoulli's principle helps explain how planes fly. It also helps explain why smoke rises up a chimney, how an atomizer works, and how a flying disk glides through the air.

- Airplane wings are curved so air moves faster over the top. There is less pressure on top of the wing. Fluid pressure pushes the airplane wing upward.

- **Lift** is an upward force due to different air pressure above and below an object.

- Wind moves air over a chimney. The air pressure is lower at the top of the chimney than at the bottom. Smoke moves up the chimney because of the different air pressure.

*Answer the following questions. Use your textbook and the ideas above.*

4. What is lift?

   a. an upward force

   b. a downward force

   c. a force that pushes to the side

5. Label the picture to show where air is moving faster and slower.

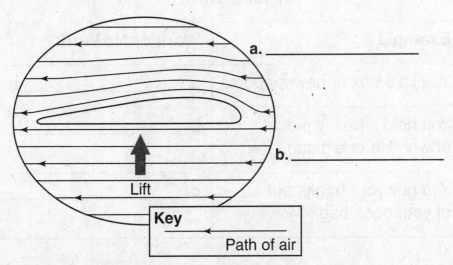

a. _____

b. _____

Lift

Key

Path of air

# What Is Work? (pages 406–411)

## The Meaning of Work (pages 406–407)

*Key Concept:* **Work is done on an object when the object moves in the same direction in which the force is exerted.**

- The word *work* has a different meaning in science than it does in everyday life. In science, **work** is when you exert a force that makes an object move in the same direction as the force.

- Work always makes an object move. If you push on a wall, the wall does not move. Even though you exert a force, there is no work done on the wall.

- The motion for work must be in the same direction as the force. If you carry books to school, the force you exert is upward. The motion of the books is toward school, so no work is done on the books.

*Answer the following questions. Use your textbook and the ideas above.*

1. Use the words *work* and *no work* to fill in the blanks in the table.

| What Is Work? | |
|---|---|
| **Example** | **Work or No Work?** |
| You lift a box of newspapers. | **a.** _____ |
| You hold a heavy piece of wood in one place. | **b.** _____ |
| You pull your books out of your book bag. | **c.** _____ |

**Work and Machines**

2. Read each word in the box. In each sentence below, fill in one of the words.

| move | force | work |
|------|-------|------|

a. Work always makes an object

_____.

b. For work to be done, the object's motion must be in

the same direction as the _____.

## Calculating Work (pages 408–409)

*Key Concept:* **The amount of work done by an object can be determined by multiplying force times distance.**

- The amount of work done on an object depends on two things: the amount of force and the distance the object moves due to the force.

- Work can be calculated using the formula:

$$\text{Work} = \text{Force} \times \text{Distance}$$

- It takes more work to move a heavy object than it does to move a light object. It takes more work to move an object a long distance than it does to move the object a short distance.

- The unit used to measure work is the **joule** (J).

*Answer the following questions. Use your textbook and the ideas above.*

3. What unit is used to measure work?

_____

**Work and Machines**

**4.** Fill in the blanks in the table. Use this formula to find the amount of work: Work = Force × Distance. Show your work in the space below.

| Calculating Work | | |
|---|---|---|
| **Amount of Force** | **Distance the Object Moves** | **How Much Work Is Done?** |
| 2 N | 3 m | 6 joules |
| 5 N | 2 m | **a.** _____ joules |
| 3 N | 1 m | **b.** _____ joules |

# Power (pages 409–411)

*Key Concept:* **Power equals the amount of work done on an object in a unit of time.**

- **Power** is a rate that tells how much work is done in a certain amount of time.

- Power can be calculated using the formula:

$$Power = \frac{Work}{Time}$$

- It takes more power to do work quickly. It takes less power to do work slowly. For example, running up a flight of stairs takes more power than walking up the same stairs.

- The unit used to measure power is the watt (W).

**Work and Machines**

*Answer the following questions. Use your textbook and the ideas on page 172.*

**5.** Read the words in the box. Use the correct words to fill in the blanks in the formula.

| Work | Time | Distance |

$$\text{Power} = \frac{\text{a. } \rule{3cm}{0.4pt}}{\text{b. } \rule{3cm}{0.4pt}}$$

**6.** Circle the item in each pair that would take more power.

| Which Takes More Power? | | |
|---|---|---|
| Walking one block | OR | Biking one block |
| Raking leaves | OR | Using a leaf blower |
| Running up stairs | OR | Walking up stairs |

**7.** Read each word in the box. In each sentence below, fill in one of the words.

| watt | joule | work |

**a.** The _____ is the unit used to measure power.

**b.** Power equals work divided by _____.

**Work and Machines**

# How Machines Do Work (pages 412–419)

## What Is a Machine? (pages 412–415)

*Key Concept:* **A machine makes work easier by changing at least one of three factors. A machine may change the amount of force you exert, the distance over which you exert your force, or the direction in which you exert your force.**

- A **machine** makes work easier. Machines can make work easier in three ways:
  1. Machines can change the amount of force.
  2. Machines can change the distance over which a force is exerted.
  3. Machines can change the direction of a force.

- The force exerted on a machine is the **input force**. The input force times the distance is the **input work**.

- The force the machine exerts on an object is the **output force**. The output force times the distance is the **output work**.

- The input work and output work are always equal. A machine cannot change the amount of work.

*Answer the following questions. Use your textbook and the ideas above.*

1. Is this sentence true or false? Machines make work easier. _____

2. Circle the letter of each way machines can make work easier.
   a. by changing the direction of a force
   b. by changing the amount of force
   c. by changing the amount of work

**3.** Read the words in the box. Use the correct words to fill in the blanks in the concept map about machines.

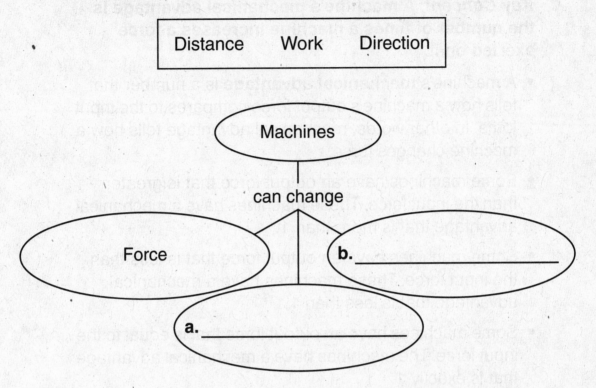

| Distance | Work | Direction |

Machines

can change

Force

b. _____

a. _____

**4.** Read the words in the box. Use the words to label the picture.

| Input force | Output force |

a. _____        b. _____

**Work and Machines**

# Mechanical Advantage (pages 416–417)

*Key Concept:* A machine's mechanical advantage is the number of times a machine increases a force exerted on it.

- A machine's **mechanical advantage** is a number that tells how a machine's output force compares to the input force. In other words, mechanical advantage tells how a machine changes force.

- Some machines have an output force that is greater than the input force. These machines have a mechanical advantage that is more than 1.

- Some machines have an output force that is less than the input force. These machines have a mechanical advantage that is less than 1.

- Some machines have an output force that is equal to the input force. The machines have a mechanical advantage that is exactly 1.

*Answer the following questions. Use your textbook and the ideas above.*

5. Read each word in the box. In each sentence below, fill in one of the words.

| more than 1 | less than 1 | exactly 1 |
|---|---|---|

    a. If a machine's output force is equal to its input force, it has a mechanical advantage of

    _____.

    b. If a machine's output force is greater than its input force, it has a mechanical advantage of

    _____.

**Work and Machines**

**6.** What is mechanical advantage?

    **a.** a number that tells how a machine changes force

    **b.** a number that tells the size of a machine

    **c.** a number that tells how fast a machine does work

## Efficiency of Machines (pages 417–419)

*Key Concept:* **To calculate the efficiency of a machine, divide the output work by the input work and multiply the result by 100 percent.**

- A machine's **efficiency** is a number that tells how the machine's output force compares to the input force. Efficiency is a percent.

- Real machines always have an efficiency that is less than 100%. That is because all real machines have some friction. Some of the input work is used to overcome friction.

- A machine with an efficiency close to 100% turns most of the input work into output work.

- A machine with a lower efficiency turns less of the input work into output work.

*Answer the following questions. Use your textbook and the ideas above.*

**7.** A number that tells how a machine's output force compares to the input force is the machine's

    _____.

**8.** Which of these machines turns the most input work into output work?

    **a.** Machine 1: Efficiency 80%

    **b.** Machine 2: Efficiency 50%

    **c.** Machine 3: Efficiency 90%

**Work and Machines**

# Simple Machines (pages 422–433)

## Inclined Plane (page 423)

*Key Concept:* **You can determine the ideal mechanical advantage of an inclined plane by dividing the length of the incline by its height.**

- An inclined plane is one kind of simple machine. An **inclined plane** is a flat, sloped surface. A ramp used to load a moving truck is an example of an inclined plane.

- An inclined plane makes work easier by increasing the distance over which a force is exerted.

- The output force of an inclined plane is greater than the input force.

*Answer the following questions. Use your textbook and the ideas above.*

1. Circle the letter of an example of an inclined plane.
   **a.** truck
   **b.** ramp
   **c.** airplane

2. Read the words in the box. Use the correct words to fill in the blanks in the concept map about inclined planes.

| Simple machines | Force | Work |
|---|---|---|

| Inclined planes | – are – | a. _____ <br><br> _____ | – that increase – | b. _____ |

**Work and Machines**

## Wedge (page 424)

*Key Concept:* **The ideal mechanical advantage of a wedge is determined by dividing the length of the wedge by its width.**

- A wedge is one kind of simple machine. A **wedge** is an inclined plane that can move.

- A wedge is thick at one end and thin at the other end. A knife is an example of a wedge.

- A wedge makes work easier by changing the direction and amount of a force.

- The longer and thinner a wedge is, the greater its mechanical advantage.

*Answer the following questions. Use your textbook and the ideas above.*

3. Is this sentence true or false? A wedge is an inclined plane that can move. _____

4. Circle the letter of the wedge with the greater mechanical advantage.

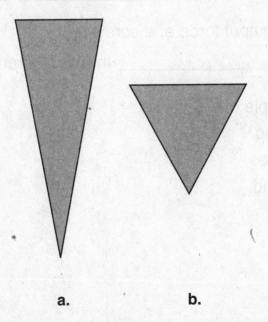

a.                              b.

**Work and Machines**

# Screws (page 425)

***Key Concept:*** **The ideal mechanical advantage of a screw is the length around the threads divided by the length of the screw.**

- A screw is one kind of simple machine. A **screw** is an inclined plane wrapped in a circle. A jar lid is an example of a screw.

- A screw makes work easier by increasing the distance over which a force is exerted.

- A screw's output force is greater than the input force.

*Answer the following questions. Use your textbook and the ideas above.*

5. An inclined plane wrapped in a circle is a(an)

   _____.

6. Read each word in the box. In the sentence below, fill in the correct words.

   | greater than | less than | equal to |
   |---|---|---|

   a. The output force of a screw is

      _____ the input force.

7. An example of a screw is
   a. a ramp.
   b. a knife.
   c. a jar lid.

**Work and Machines**

## Levers (pages 426–427)

*Key Concept:* **The ideal mechanical advantage of a lever is determined by dividing the distance from the fulcrum to the input force by the distance from the fulcrum to the output force.**

- A lever is one kind of simple machine. A **lever** is a bar that moves around a fixed point called a **fulcrum**. There are three kinds, or classes, of levers.

- In a first-class lever, the fulcrum is between the input force and output force. First-class levers change the direction of a force. A seesaw is a first-class lever.

- In a second-class lever, the output force is between the fulcrum and the input force. Second-class levers increase a force. A wheelbarrow is a second-class lever.

- In a third-class lever, the input force is between the fulcrum and the output force. Third-class levers increase the distance over which a force is exerted. A hockey stick is a third-class lever.

*Answer the following questions. Use your textbook and the ideas above.*

**8.** Draw a line from each term to its meaning.

| Term | Meaning |
|------|---------|
| fulcrum | **a.** a bar that moves |
| lever | **b.** a fixed point |

**9.** Circle the letter of each example of a lever.
   a. hockey stick
   b. screw
   c. wheelbarrow

**Work and Machines**

**10.** Read the words in the box. Use the correct words
to label the diagram.

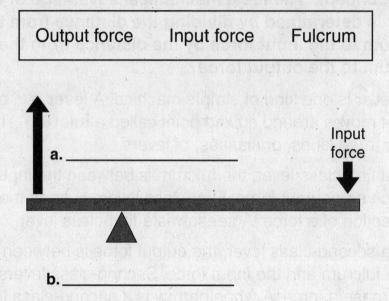

| Output force | Input force | Fulcrum |

## Wheel and Axle (pages 428–430)

*Key Concept:* **You can find the mechanical advantage
of a wheel and axle by dividing the radius of the wheel
by the radius of the axle.**

- A wheel and axle is one kind of simple machine. A
  **wheel and axle** is two circular objects that are joined
  together. A screwdriver and a doorknob are examples of
  wheel and axles.

- Some wheel and axles increase force. Other wheel and
  axles increase the distance over which a force is
  exerted.

*Answer the following questions. Use your textbook and the
ideas above.*

**11.** Circle the letter of each example of a wheel and axle.

    **a.** doorknob

    **b.** screwdriver

    **c.** screw

**12.** Circle each way a wheel and axle can help you do work.

    **a.** reduce the work

    **b.** increase the force

    **c.** increase the distance over which a force is exerted

## Pulley (pages 430–431)

*Key Concept:* **The ideal mechanical advantage of a pulley is equal to the number of sections of rope that support the object.**

- A pulley is one kind of simple machine. A **pulley** is a wheel with a rope or cable wrapped around it. A pulley is used to raise a flag on a flagpole.

- Pulleys can change the amount or direction of the input force.

*Answer the following questions. Use your textbook and the ideas above.*

**13.** Is this sentence true or false? A pulley changes the amount of work needed to raise a flag. _____

**14.** You can use a(an) _____ to raise a flag up a flagpole.

## Simple Machines in the Body (page 432)

*Key Concept:* **Most of the machines in your body are levers that consist of bones and muscles.**

- Levers are found in your body. Your arm works as a lever when you bend your elbow. Your foot acts as a lever when you take a step.

- Wedges are found in your body, too. Your front teeth are wedges that help you bite through food.

**Work and Machines**

*Answer the following questions. Use your textbook and the ideas on page 183.*

**15.** When you bend your knee, your leg acts as a
   **a.** wedge.
   **b.** lever.
   **c.** pulley.

**16.** When you bite into an apple, your front teeth act as
   **a.** wedges.
   **b.** levers.
   **c.** pulleys.

# Compound Machines (page 433)

*Key Concept:* **The ideal mechanical advantage of a compound machine is the product of the individual ideal mechanical advantages of the simple machines that make it up.**

- A **compound machine** is made of two or more simple machines.

- Most machines you use are compound machines. A bicycle is one example of a compound machine.

*Answer the following questions. Use your textbook and the ideas above.*

**17.** A machine that is made of two or more simple machines is called a(an) _____.

**18.** Is the following sentence true or false? A bicycle is an example of a simple machine. _____

# What Is Energy? (pages 442–446)

## Energy, Work, and Power (page 443)

*Key Concept:* If the transfer of energy is work, then power is the rate at which energy is transferred, or the amount of energy transferred in a unit of time.

- When a force moves an object, work is done. **Energy** is the ability to do work.

- When work is done on an object, some energy transfers to that object.

- Power tells how much energy is transferred in each unit of time. The formula for power is:

$$\text{Power} = \frac{\text{Energy transferred}}{\text{Time}}$$

*Answer the following questions. Use your textbook and the ideas above.*

1. Draw a line from each term to its meaning.

| Term | Meaning |
|---|---|
| work | **a.** amount of energy transferred in each unit of time |
| energy | |
| | **b.** the ability to do work |
| power | **c.** when a force causes motion |

2. Is the following sentence true or false? Force is the ability to do work. _____

## Kinetic Energy (pages 443–444)

***Key Concept:*** **Two basic kinds of energy are kinetic energy and potential energy.**

- **Kinetic energy** is energy of motion.

- The amount of kinetic energy an object has depends on its mass and its velocity.

- The faster an object moves, the more kinetic energy it has. The more mass an object has, the more kinetic energy it has.

*Answer the following questions. Use your textbook and the ideas above.*

3. The energy of motion is called

   _____.

4. Read the words in the box. Use the words to fill in the blanks in the concept map about kinetic energy.

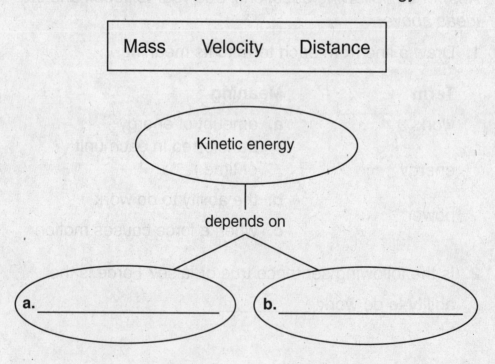

Energy

## Potential Energy (pages 445–446)

***Key Concept:*** **Two basic kinds of energy are kinetic energy and potential energy.**

- **Potential energy** is stored energy. Energy can be stored in an object because of where it is or because of its shape.

- A book sitting on a desk has potential energy. Energy was stored in the book when it was lifted onto the desk. Potential energy due to an object's height is called **gravitational potential energy**. The greater an object's height, the more gravitational potential energy it has. The greater an object's weight, the more gravitational potential energy it has.

- **Elastic potential energy** is the energy in springs and archery bows.

*Answer the following questions. Use your textbook and the ideas above.*

5. Stored energy is called _____.

6. Read each word in the box. In each sentence below, fill in the correct word or words.

> gravitational potential       kinetic
>
> elastic potential

   a. A stretched rubber band has

   _____ energy.

   b. A book on top of a desk has

   _____ energy.

**Energy**

*Use the pictures to answer questions 7 and 8.*

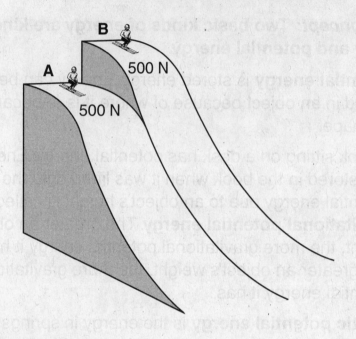

7. Both skiers above weigh 500 N. Which skier, A or B, has more gravitational potential energy? _____

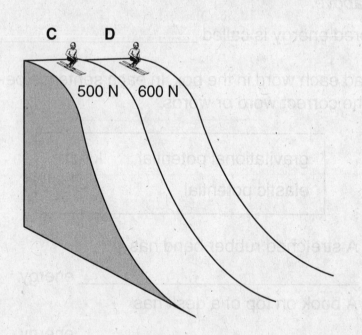

8. Skier C above weighs 500 N. Skier D weighs 600 N. Which skier, C or D, has more gravitational potential energy? _____

# Forms of Energy (pages 447–451)

## Mechanical Energy (pages 447–448)

*Key Concept:* **You can find an object's mechanical energy by adding the object's kinetic energy and potential energy.**

- **Mechanical energy** is the energy an object has because of its position and its motion.

- You can find an object's mechanical energy by adding its kinetic energy and its potential energy. Use this formula:

$$\text{Mechanical energy} = \text{Potential energy} + \text{Kinetic energy}$$

*Answer the following questions. Use your textbook and the ideas above.*

1. Read the words in the box. Use the words to fill in the blanks in the concept map about mechanical energy.

| Kinetic energy | Position | Potential energy |
|---|---|---|

Mechanical energy

is a combination of

and

a. _____

b. _____

2. Circle the letter of the formula for mechanical energy.

   **a.** Mechanical energy = Potential energy − Kinetic energy

   **b.** Mechanical energy = Potential energy + Kinetic energy

   **c.** Mechanical energy = Potential energy × Kinetic energy

## Other Forms of Energy (pages 449–451)

*Key Concept:* **Forms of energy associated with the particles of objects include thermal energy, electrical energy, chemical energy, nuclear energy, and electromagnetic energy.**

- **Thermal energy** is the total energy in the particles of an object. Hot things have more thermal energy than cold things.

- **Electrical energy** is the energy of electrical charges. Lightning is a form of electrical energy.

- **Chemical energy** is the energy in chemical bonds. Your body uses the chemical energy in food.

- **Nuclear energy** is the energy stored in the nuclei of atoms. Nuclear power plants use nuclear energy to make electricity.

- **Electromagnetic energy** travels in waves. X-rays and microwaves are electromagnetic energy.

*Answer the following questions. Use your textbook and the ideas above.*

3. Is the following sentence true or false? The particles of objects cannot have energy. _____

Name _____  Date _____  Class _____

4.  Read the words in the box. Use the words to fill in the blanks in the table about forms of energy.

| Thermal energy | Chemical energy |
|---|---|
| Nuclear energy | Electromagnetic energy |
| Electrical energy | |

| Type of Energy | Description |
|---|---|
| Thermal energy | total energy of the particles in an object |
| a. _____ _____ | energy stored in the nuclei of atoms |
| b. _____ _____ | energy in chemical bonds |
| c. _____ _____ | travels in waves |
| d. _____ _____ | energy of electrical changes |

**Energy**

# Energy Transformations and Conservation (pages 454–459)

## Energy Transformations (pages 454–455)

*Key Concept:* **Most forms of energy can be transformed into other forms.**

- Energy can change forms. An **energy transformation** is a change from one form of energy to another form of energy.

- Energy transformations happen all around you. A toaster changes electrical energy to thermal energy. Your body changes the chemical energy in food to mechanical energy as you move.

- Sometimes energy changes forms once to do work. These are single transformations.

- Sometimes energy changes forms several times to do work. These are multiple transformations.

*Answer the following questions. Use your textbook and the ideas above.*

1. Is this sentence true or false? Energy never changes

   forms. _____

2. In each sentence below, fill in the correct word.

   a. When a toaster changes electrical energy to

      thermal energy, it is a(an) _____
      transformation.

   b. A car's engine changes the form of energy

      several times. This is a(an) _____
      transformation.

**Energy**

# Transformations Between Potential and Kinetic Energy (pages 456–457)

***Key Concept:*** **One of the most common energy transformations is the transformation between potential energy and kinetic energy.**

- Kinetic energy is the energy of motion. Potential energy is stored energy. Energy can change from potential to kinetic and back again.

- Energy changes form when an object moves up or down. The object has the most potential energy at its highest point. The object has the most kinetic energy at its lowest point.

- A pendulum changes energy as it swings. It has the most potential energy at its highest point. It has the most kinetic energy at its lowest point.

*Answer the following questions. Use your textbook and the ideas above.*

*Use the picture to answer questions 3 and 4.*

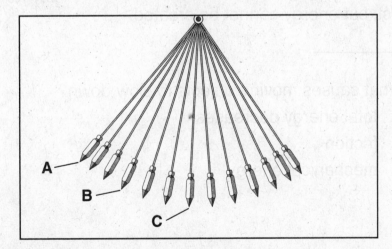

3. At what point does the pendulum have the greatest potential energy? _____

4. At what point does the pendulum have the greatest kinetic energy? _____

# Conservation of Energy (pages 458–459)

*Key Concept:* According to the law of conservation of energy, energy cannot be created or destroyed.

• The amount of energy does not change when energy changes forms. Energy is not lost. Energy is not created. This is the **law of conservation of energy**.

• Energy is not lost when a moving object slows down. Friction changes mechanical energy to thermal energy.

• For example, a spinning top slows down because of friction. Friction with the floor and friction with the air changes some of the top's mechanical energy to thermal energy.

• Energy can be created if matter is destroyed. **Matter** is anything that has mass. A tiny bit of matter can make a huge amount of energy.

*Answer the following questions. Use your textbook and the ideas above.*

5. Is the following sentence true or false? Energy can be lost, but energy cannot be created.

_____

6. What causes moving objects to slow down?
   a. total energy decreases
   b. friction
   c. mechanical energy

7. Read the words in the box. Use the words to fill in the blanks in the concept map about the conservation of energy.

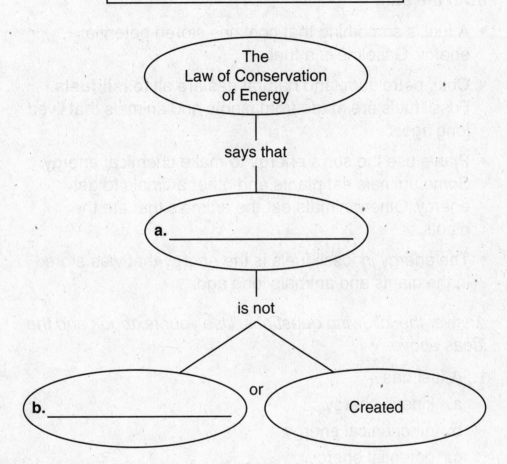

Energy    Lost    Transformed

The Law of Conservation of Energy

says that

a. _____

is not

b. _____  or  Created

**Energy**

# Energy and Fossil Fuels (pages 462–465)

## Formation of Fossil Fuels (pages 462–464)

*Key Concept:* Fossil fuels contain energy that came from the sun.

- A fuel is something that contains stored potential energy. Gasoline is a fuel.

- Coal, petroleum, and natural gas are all **fossil fuels**. Fossil fuels are made from plants and animals that lived long ago.

- Plants use the sun's energy to make chemical energy. Some animals eat plants and other animals to get energy. Other animals eat the animals that ate the plants.

- The energy in fossil fuels is the energy that was stored in the plants and animals long ago.

*Answer the following questions. Use your textbook and the ideas above.*

1. A fuel has
   a. kinetic energy.
   b. mechanical energy.
   c. potential energy.

2. Where did the energy in fossil fuels originally come from?
   a. the sun
   b. animals
   c. fossils

3. Read each word in the box. In each sentence below, fill in the correct word or words.

| fossil fuels | potential energy | sunlight |
|---|---|---|

   a. The energy in a fuel is _____.

   b. The energy in _____ is the energy from plants and animals long ago.

4. Circle the letter of each fossil fuel.

   a. wood

   b. natural gas

   c. coal

## Use of Fossil Fuels (pages 464–465)

*Key Concept:* **Fossil fuels can be burned to release the chemical energy stored millions of years ago.**

- **Combustion** means burning. During combustion, chemical energy is changed to thermal energy.

- A fossil fuel is burned at a power plant. The chemical energy in the fossil fuel is changed to thermal energy. The thermal energy heats water to make steam. The steam turns a turbine. The turbine changes thermal energy to mechanical energy. A generator changes mechanical energy to electrical energy. The electrical energy is used in homes and businesses to do work.

*Answer the following questions. Use your textbook and the ideas above.*

5. Chemical energy is changed to thermal energy during

   _____.

**Energy**

6. Read the words in the box. Use the correct words to fill in the blanks in the flowchart about energy transformations at a power plant.

| |
|---|
| thermal energy      electrical energy<br><br>mechanical energy |

| |
|---|
| Fossil fuels are burned at a power plant. |

↓

| |
|---|
| Chemical energy is changed to  a._____<br><br>_____ |

↓

| |
|---|
| Thermal energy is used to heat water and make steam. |

↓

| |
|---|
| Steam turns a turbine, which changes thermal energy to<br><br>b._____ . |

↓

| |
|---|
| A generator changes mechanical energy to<br><br>c._____ . |

**Thermal Energy and Heat**

# Temperature, Thermal Energy, and Heat (pages 472–477)

## Temperature (pages 472–474)

***Key Concept:*** **The three common scales for measuring temperature are the Fahrenheit, Celsius, and Kelvin scales.**

- All objects are made up of tiny particles. **Temperature** tells how quickly the particles in an object are moving.

- The particles in a warm object move quickly. The object has a high temperature. The particles in a cool object move slowly. The object has a low temperature.

- A thermometer measures temperature. A thermometer contains liquid. The level of the liquid tells the temperature.

- There are three temperature scales that are commonly used. On the **Fahrenheit scale**, water freezes at 32°F and boils at 212°F. On the **Celsius scale**, water freezes at 0°C and boils at 100°C. On the **Kelvin scale**, water freezes at 273 K and boils at 373 K.

*Answer the following questions. Use your textbook and the ideas above.*

1. A measure of how quickly the particles in an object are moving is _____.

2. Which of these has the fastest-moving particles?
   a. an ice cube
   b. a cup of cold water
   c. a mug of boiling water

**Thermal Energy and Heat**

**3.** A tool used to measure temperature is an(an)

_____.

**4.** Read the words in the box. Use the words to fill in the
blanks in the table about temperature scales.

| Fahrenheit | Celsius | Kelvin |
|---|---|---|

| Temperature | | |
|---|---|---|
| **Scale** | **Water Freezes** | **Water Boils** |
| a. _____ | 273 | 373 |
| b. _____ | 0°C | 100°C |
| c. _____ | 32°F | 212°F |

**5.** Is the following sentence true or false? The particles in
a cool object move more quickly than the particles

in a warm object. _____

# Thermal Energy and Heat (pages 474–475)

***Key Concept:*** **Heat is thermal energy moving from a warmer object to a cooler object.**

- Thermal energy is the total energy of all the particles in an object.

- Thermal energy depends on how fast the particles are moving. Thermal energy also depends on how many particles there are. That is why a liter of hot water has more thermal energy than a drop of water at the same temperature.

- **Heat** is moving thermal energy. Heat always moves from a warmer object to a cooler object.

*Answer the following questions. Use your textbook and the ideas above.*

6. Circle the letters of two things that determine how much thermal energy an object has.

    a. how many particles it has

    b. which temperature scale is used

    c. how fast its particles are moving

7. Thermal energy that moves from a warmer object to a cooler object is called _____.

8. Draw arrows in the picture to show in which direction heat moves.

**Thermal Energy and Heat**

# Specific Heat (pages 476–477)

*Key Concept:* **A material with a high specific heat can absorb a great deal of thermal energy without a great change in temperature.**

- When an object is heated, its temperature rises. How much its temperature rises depends on its specific heat.

- **Specific heat** is the amount of energy needed to raise the temperature of 1 kilogram of a material by 1 kelvin.

- Different materials have different specific heats. Water has a high specific heat. It takes a lot of energy to raise the temperature of water. Silver has a low specific heat. It does not take much energy to raise the temperature of silver.

*Answer the following question. Use your textbook and the ideas above.*

9. Use the table to answer the question. If one kilogram of each of these materials absorbed the same amount of energy, which material would have the biggest change

   in temperature? _____

| Specific Heat of Some Materials | |
|---|---|
| **Material** | **Specific Heat (J/ kg·K)** |
| Glass | 837 |
| Iron | 450 |
| Sand | 800 |

**Thermal Energy and Heat**

# The Transfer of Heat (pages 479–483)

## How Is Heat Transferred? (pages 480–481)

*Key Concept:* **Heat is transferred by conduction, convection, and radiation.**

- There are three ways that heat can move: conduction, convection, and radiation.

- **Conduction** is heat moving from one particle to another. A metal spoon in hot soup gets warm because of conduction. Conduction happens between objects that are touching.

- **Convection** is heat transfer in a moving fluid. Gases and liquids are fluids. When a fluid is heated, it moves. The moving fluid transfers heat.

- **Radiation** is energy transfer by electromagnetic waves. The sun's energy travels to Earth by radiation. Matter is not needed for the transfer of energy by radiation.

*Answer the following questions. Use your textbook and the ideas above.*

1. Fill in the blanks in the table about heat transfer.

| Heat Transfer | |
| --- | --- |
| **Process** | **How Heat Moves** |
| a. _____ | in a moving fluid |
| b. _____ | from one particle to another |
| c. _____ | by electromagnetic waves |

**Thermal Energy and Heat**

2. Which kind of heat transfer does not need matter?
   a. conduction
   b. convection
   c. radiation

3. Read each word in the box. In each sentence below, fill in one of the words.

   | conduction | convection | radiation |
   |---|---|---|

   a. Energy moves in a pot of boiling water due to

      _____.

   b. The sun's energy travels to Earth by

      _____.

   c. A metal spoon gets warm in a bowl of hot soup

      due to _____.

# Heat Moves One Way (page 482)

***Key Concept:* If two objects have different temperatures, heat will flow from the warmer object to the colder one.**

- Heat can move in only one way. Heat always moves from a warmer object to a colder one.

- Heat will move between two objects until they are the same temperature.

*Answer the following question. Use your textbook and the ideas above.*

4. Read the words in the box. Use the words to fill in the blanks in the flowchart about heat.

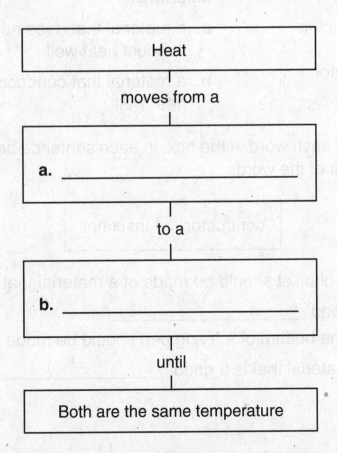

| Cooler object | Conduction | Warmer object |

Heat

moves from a

a. _____

to a

b. _____

until

Both are the same temperature

# Conductors and Insulators (pages 482–483)

*Key Concept:* **A conductor transfers thermal energy well. An insulator does not transfer thermal energy well.**

- A **conductor** is a material that transfers heat energy well. Metals are good conductors. A material that is a good conductor feels cool when you touch it. That is because a conductor easily transfers heat away from your body.

- An **insulator** is a material that does not conduct heat well. Wood and air are good insulators.

*Answer the following questions. Use your textbook and the ideas above.*

**5.** Draw a line from each term to its meaning.

| Term | Meaning |
|------|---------|
| conductor | **a.** a material that does not conduct heat well |
| insulator | **b.** a material that conducts heat well |

**6.** Read each word in the box. In each sentence below, fill in one of the words.

> conductor    insulator

**a.** A blanket should be made of a material that is a good _____.

**b.** The bottom of a frying pan should be made of a material that is a good _____.

# Thermal Energy and States of Matter (pages 486–490)

## States of Matter (page 487)

***Key Concept:*** **Most matter on Earth can exist in three states—solid, liquid, and gas.**

- Most matter on Earth is a solid, a liquid, or a gas. These three forms of matter are called **states**.

- The particles in a solid are packed together. They cannot move out of their places. That is why a solid does not change shape.

- The particles in a liquid are close together. They can move around, though. That is why a liquid can flow.

- The particles in a gas move very fast. They do not stay close together. That is why a gas spreads out and fills its container.

*Answer the following questions. Use your textbook and the ideas above.*

1.  Read each word in the box. In each sentence below, fill in one of the words.

|  |  |  |
|---|---|---|
| gas | solid | liquid |

a. The particles in a _____ do not change positions.

b. The particles in a _____ move very quickly.

c. The particles in a _____ are close together but can move around.

**Thermal Energy and Heat**

2. Read the words in the box. Use the words to label the
   pictures.

| solid | gas |
|-------|-----|

**Liquid**

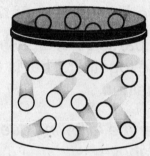

a. _____

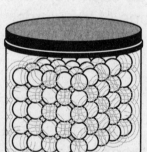

b. _____

# Changes of State (pages 488–489)

***Key Concept:*** Matter can change from one state to another when thermal energy is absorbed or released.

- A **change of state** is a change from one state of matter to another state of matter.

- A change from a solid to a liquid is called **melting**. An object absorbs thermal energy when it melts.

- A change from a liquid to a solid is called **freezing**. An object looses thermal energy when it freezes.

- A change from a liquid to a gas is called vaporization. During vaporization, a liquid absorbs thermal energy.

- When vaporization happens at the surface of a liquid, it is called **evaporation**. This is what causes puddles to dry up. At higher temperatures, vaporization can happen below the surface of the liquid. This is called **boiling**.

- A change from a gas to a liquid is called **condensation**. During condensation, a gas looses thermal energy.

*Answer the following questions. Use your textbook and the ideas above.*

3. A change from one state of matter to another state of matter is a(an) _____.

4. Draw a line from each term to its meaning.

| Term | Meaning |
|------|---------|
| freezing | **a.** a change from a liquid to a solid |
| melting | **b.** a change from a gas to a liquid |
| condensation | **c.** a change from a solid to a liquid |

**Thermal Energy and Heat**

# Thermal Expansion (page 490)

*Key Concept:* **As the thermal energy of matter increases, its particles spread out and the substance expands.**

- When an object is heated, it gets bigger. The particles in the object move apart from each other. This is called **thermal expansion**.

- When an object is cooled, it gets smaller. The particles in the object move closer together.

- A thermostat is a device that is used to turn heating systems on and off. A thermostat works because of thermal expansion.

*Answer the following questions. Use your textbook and the ideas above.*

5. When an object is heated and it gets bigger, it is called

   _____.

6. Circle the letter of each sentence that is true about thermal expansion.

   a. The particles in an object move apart when the object is heated.

   b. An object gets smaller as it gets warmer.

   c. A thermostat works because of thermal expansion.

# Uses of Heat (pages 491–495)

## Heat Engines (pages 491–493)

*Key Concept:* **Heat engines transform thermal energy to mechanical energy.**

- A **heat engine** changes thermal energy to mechanical energy. There are two kinds of heat engines: external combustion engines and internal combustion engines.

- **External combustion engines** burn fuel outside the engine. A steam engine is an example.

- **Internal combustion engines** burn fuel inside the engine. Cars and trucks use internal combustion engines.

*Answer the following questions. Use your textbook and the ideas above.*

1. Draw a line from each term to its meaning.

| Term | Meaning |
|---|---|
| internal combustion engine | **a.** an engine that burns fuel inside of the engine |
| heat engine | **b.** an engine that burns fuel outside of the engine |
| external combustion engine | **c.** any engine that changes thermal energy to mechanical energy |

2. Read each word in the box. In each sentence below, fill in one of the words.

> car engine     steam engine

    **a.** An example of an external combustion engine is a _____.

    **b.** An example of an internal combustion engine is a _____.

## Cooling Systems (pages 494–495)

*Key Concept:* **A refrigerator is a device that transfers thermal energy from inside the refrigerator to the room outside.**

- A cooling system transfers heat to keep things cool.

- A refrigerator is one kind of cooling system. A **refrigerant** is a material used in a refrigerator. A refrigerant absorbs and releases heat.

- An air conditioner is another kind of cooling system. Air conditioners are used to keep buildings and cars cool.

*Answer the following questions. Use your textbook and the ideas above.*

3. Circle the letter of each sentence that is true about cooling systems.

    **a.** Cooling systems transfer heat.

    **b.** A car engine is an example of a cooling system.

    **c.** Cooling systems use refrigerants to transfer heat.

**Thermal Energy and Heat**

**4.** Read the words in the box. Use the words to fill in the blanks in the flowchart about cooling systems.

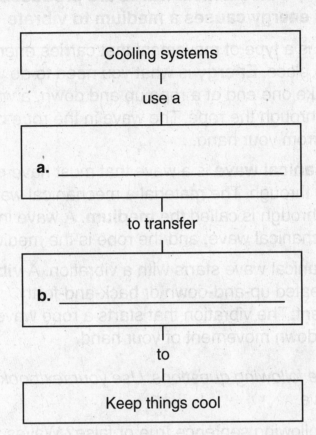

| Heat | Refrigerator | Refrigerant |

Cooling systems

use a

a. _____

to transfer

b. _____

to

Keep things cool

# What Are Waves? (pages 510–514)

## Waves and Energy (pages 511–512)

*Key Concept:* **Mechanical waves are produced when a source of energy causes a medium to vibrate.**

- A **wave** is a type of movement that carries energy from place to place. **Energy** is what you need to do work. If you shake one end of a rope up and down, a wave travels through the rope. The wave in the rope carries energy from your hand.

- A **mechanical wave** is a wave that must have material to travel through. The material a mechanical wave travels through is called the **medium**. A wave in a rope is a mechanical wave, and the rope is the medium.

- A mechanical wave starts with a vibration. A **vibration** is a repeated up-and-down or back-and-forth movement. The vibration that starts a rope wave is the up-and-down movement of your hand.

*Answer the following questions. Use your textbook and the ideas above.*

1. Is the following sentence true or false? Waves that must have material, such as rope, to travel through are called mechanical waves. _____

2. Is the following sentence true or false? A wave carries the medium from place to place. _____

**Characteristics of Waves**

3. Read the words in the box. In each sentence below, fill in one of the words.

> wave     medium     energy
>
> vibration

a. A repeated up-and-down or back-and-forth

movement is a(an) _____.

b. A type of movement that carries energy from place

to place is a(an) _____.

c. The material a mechanical wave travels through is

called the _____.

## Types of Waves (pages 512–514)

*Key Concept:* **Mechanical waves are classified by how they move. There are two types of mechanical waves: transverse waves and longitudinal waves.**

- **Transverse waves** move the medium up and down. A wave in a rope is a transverse wave.

- **Longitudinal** (lawn juh TOO duh nul) **waves** move the medium back and forth. A wave in a spring toy is a longitudinal wave.

Characteristics of Waves

Name _____ Date _____ Class _____

**Characteristics of Waves**

*Answer the following questions. Use your textbook and the ideas on page 215.*

4. Fill in the blanks in the table about types of mechanical waves.

| Types of Mechanical Waves | | |
| --- | --- | --- |
| **Type of Wave** | **How it moves the Medium** | **Example** |
| Transverse | a. _____ _____ | wave in a rope |
| b. _____ | back and forth | slower |

5. The pictures show a transverse wave and a longitudinal wave. Which is the transverse wave, and which is the longitudinal wave?

   a. _____

   b. _____

a.

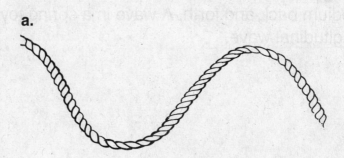

b.

# Properties of Waves

**(pages 515–519)**

## Amplitude (page 516)

*Key Concept:* **Amplitude is one basic property of waves.**

- **Amplitude** is how far the medium moves when a wave passes through it.

- For a transverse wave, amplitude is how far the medium moves up or down. For a longitudinal wave, amplitude is how far the medium moves back or forth.

- Amplitude shows how much energy a wave has. The more energy a wave has, the bigger the amplitude of the wave.

*Answer the following questions. Use your textbook and the ideas above.*

**1.** Circle the letter of the choice that correctly describes the amplitude of a transverse wave.

    **a.** how fast the medium moves back and forth

    **b.** how far the medium moves up or down

    **c.** how far the medium moves back and forth

**2.** Is the following sentence true or false? Amplitude shows how much energy a wave has. _____

## Wavelength (page 517)

***Key Concept: Wavelength is a basic property of waves.***

- **Wavelength** is how far a wave travels before it starts to repeat.

- To find the wavelength of a transverse wave, you can measure the distance between the top of one wave and the top of the next wave. Or, you can measure the distance between the bottom of one wave and the bottom of the next wave.

*Answer the following questions. Use your textbook and the ideas above.*

3. The distance a wave travels before it starts to repeat is the _____.

4. The picture shows a transverse wave. Which arrow shows the wavelength? _____

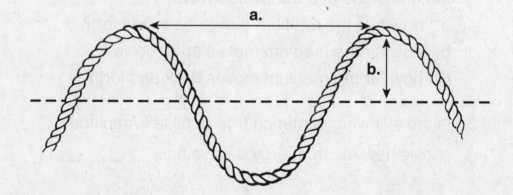

# Frequency (page 517)

*Key Concept:* **Frequency is a basic property of waves.**

- **Frequency** is the number of waves that go by a point in a certain amount of time.

- Suppose water waves are moving past a post. If one wave passes the post each second, the frequency of the waves is one wave per second.

- Frequency is measured in units called **hertz** (Hz). If one wave passes a point each second, the frequency is 1 Hz. If two waves pass a point each second, the frequency is 2 Hz.

*Answer the following questions. Use your textbook and the ideas above.*

5. The number of waves that go by a point in a certain amount of time is the _____.

6. If three waves pass a point in one second, what is the frequency of the waves? Circle the letter of the correct answer.
   a. 1/3 Hz
   b. 1 Hz
   c. 3 Hz

# Speed (pages 518–519)

*Key Concept:* **Speed is a basic property of waves. The speed, wavelength, and frequency of a wave are related to one another by a mathematical formula:**

### Speed = Wavelength × Frequency

- Speed is how far a wave travels in a given amount of time. For example, if a wave travels 5 cm in 1 second, its speed is 5 cm per second.

**Characteristics of Waves**

- To find the speed of a wave, you can multiply the wavelength times the frequency. Suppose the wavelength is 4 cm and the frequency is 1 wave per second. Then the speed is 4 cm × 1 per second, or 4 cm per second.

*Answer the following questions. Use your textbook and the ideas on page 219 and above.*

**7.** Is the following sentence true or false? The distance a wave travels in a given amount of time is the frequency.

_____

**8.** Fill in the blank in the concept map about wave speed.

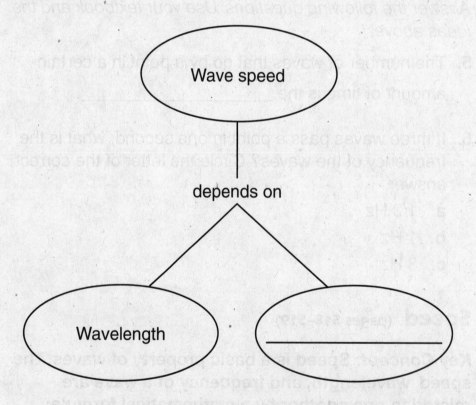

**9.** If a wave has a wavelength of 2 m and a frequency of 1 wave per second, what is the speed of the wave? Circle the letter of the correct answer.

**a.** 2 m per second

**b.** 1 m per second

**c.** 0.5 m per second

# Interactions of Waves

**(pages 521–527)**

## Reflection (page 522)

*Key Concept:* **When an object or a wave hits a surface through which it cannot pass, it bounces back.**

- **Reflection** is the bouncing back of a wave or object from a surface. For example, if you throw a ball at a wall, the ball bounces back. The ball is reflected by the wall.

- Sound waves bounce off walls and other hard surfaces. Reflected sound waves are called echoes.

- Light waves bounce off mirrors and other shiny surfaces. You see your face in a mirror because light from your face bounces back from the mirror to your eyes.

*Answer the following questions. Use your textbook and the ideas above.*

1. The bouncing back of a wave or object from a surface is called _____.

2. Circle the letter of an example of reflection.

   **a.** a pitcher throwing a ball

   **b.** a rocket flying into space

   **c.** an echo

3. Is the following sentence true or false? You can see yourself in a mirror because of reflection. _____

**Characteristics of Waves**

# Refraction (page 523)

***Key Concept:*** **When a wave enters a new medium at an angle, one side of the wave changes speed before the other side, causing the wave to bend.**

- **Refraction** is the bending of a wave due to a change in speed. Refraction happens only when a wave enters a new medium at an angle.

- Light travels slower through water than through air. So, when light enters water, it slows down.

- If a light wave passes from air into water at an angle, one side of the light wave enters the water before the other side. This causes the light wave to bend.

*Answer the following questions. Use your textbook and the ideas above.*

4. Is the following sentence true or false? Reflection happens only when a wave enters a new medium at an angle. _____

5. The pictures show light waves moving from air into water. Which picture shows refraction? _____

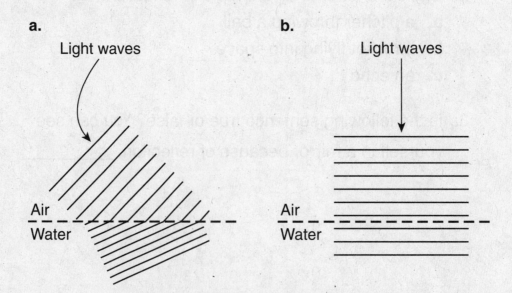

a. Light waves

b. Light waves

Air

Water

Air

Water

## Diffraction (page 524)

**Key Concept:** When a wave moves around a barrier or through an opening in a barrier, it bends and spreads out.

- **Diffraction** is the bending and spreading out of waves. Diffraction happens when waves go around a barrier or through a hole in a barrier.

- Suppose that ocean waves hit a big ship. The ship is a barrier to the waves. The waves bend to travel around the ship. Then, the waves spread out across the water on the other side of the ship. The waves have been diffracted.

*Answer the following questions. Use your textbook and the ideas above.*

6. Is the following sentence true or false? The bending and spreading out of waves when they go around a

   barrier is called refraction. _____

7. The picture shows water waves reaching a hole in a wall. What will happen to the waves after they go

   through the hole?_____
   a. The waves will bend and spread apart.
   b. The waves will not change.
   c. The waves will become smaller.

Water waves
↓

_____
_____
_____
━━━━━━━━━━━━━━━        ┝━━━━━━━━━━━━━ Wall

**Characteristics of Waves**

# Interference (pages 524–525)

***Key Concept:*** **There are two types of interference: constructive and destructive.**

- **Interference** is what happens between waves that bump into one another. When waves interfere, the waves combine to form a single wave.

- **Constructive interference** happens when the high points of one wave pass through the high points of another wave. The two waves combine to make a wave with a larger amplitude.

- **Destructive interference** happens when the high points of one wave pass through the low points of another wave. The two waves combine to make a wave with a smaller amplitude.

*Answer the following questions. Use your textbook and the ideas above.*

8. Is the following sentence true or false? Interference is what happens between waves that bump into one another. _____

9. Fill in the blanks in the table about types of interference.

| Types of Interference | |
|---|---|
| **Type of Interference** | **Amplitude of Combined Wave** |
| Constructive | a. _____ |
| b. _____ | smaller |

# Standing Waves (pages 526–527)

***Key Concept:*** **If the incoming wave and a reflected wave have just the right frequency, they produce a combined wave that appears to be standing still.**

- A **standing wave** is a wave that seems to stand in one place. A standing wave is really two waves interfering with one another.

- If you tie one end of a rope to a doorknob and shake the other end of the rope up and down, waves travel through the rope to the doorknob. At the doorknob, the waves reflect and travel back toward your hand. The waves you are making and the reflected waves pass through each other. They combine to make a single wave. If the waves have just the right frequency, the combined wave seems to be standing still.

*Answer the following question. Use your textbook and the ideas above.*

**10.** Circle the letter of the sentence that is true about standing waves.

    **a.** They are waves that do not move.

    **b.** They are caused by interference.

    **c.** They are waves that are moving so slowly that they seem to be standing still.

# Seismic Waves (pages 530–533)

## Types of Seismic Waves (pages 531–532)

**Key Concept:** Seismic waves include P waves, S waves, and surface waves.

- Earthquakes cause waves that move through the ground. Earthquake waves are called **seismic waves**.

- **P waves** are longitudinal waves. P waves move more quickly than other types of seismic waves.

- **S waves** are transverse waves. S waves cannot travel through liquids, including Earth's core.

- **Surface waves** are a combination of longitudinal and transverse waves. Surface waves move more slowly than P waves or S waves. They also cause more damage than P waves or S waves.

- **Tsunamis** (tsoo NAH meez) are huge surface waves in oceans. They are caused by underwater earthquakes.

*Answer the following questions. Use your textbook and the ideas above.*

1. Read the words in the box. In each sentence below, fill in the correct word or words.

   | P wave | tsunami | S wave |
   | surface wave | | |

   a. The type of seismic wave that travels the fastest is a _____.

   b. The type of seismic wave that does the most damage is a _____.

   c. The type of seismic wave that cannot travel through liquids is a _____.

**2.** Is the following sentence true or false? Earthquakes cause seismic waves. _____

**3.** Huge surface waves in ocean water are called _____.

## Detecting Seismic Waves (page 533)

*Key Concept:* **A seismograph records the ground movements caused by seismic waves as they move through Earth.**

- **Seismographs** (SYZ muh grafs) are instruments that measure earthquake waves.

- Seismographs can be used to find where an earthquake happened. Seismographs can also be used to find underground resources, such as oil and water.

*Answer the following questions. Use your textbook and the ideas above.*

**4.** Circle the letter of what a seismograph measures.

    **a.** earthquake waves

    **b.** sound waves

    **c.** light waves

**5.** Is the following sentence true or false? Seismographs can be used to find underground resources. _____

# The Nature of Sound

**(pages 540–545)**

## Sound Waves (pages 540–541)

*Key Concept:* **Sound is a disturbance that travels through a medium as a longitudinal wave.**

- Sound waves are longitudinal waves. They begin with a back-and-forth vibration.

- If you pluck a guitar string, it vibrates back and forth. The vibrating string sends a longitudinal wave through the air.

- Sound waves need a medium to travel through. Sound waves can travel through gases such as air. They can also travel through liquids such as water and solids such as wood. You might hear a car horn when you are indoors because sound waves can travel through solid walls.

*Answer the following questions. Use your textbook and the ideas above.*

1. Circle the letter of the type of wave a sound wave is.
   a. transverse wave
   b. longitudinal wave
   c. combined wave

2. Is the following sentence true or false? Sound waves can travel only through air. _____

Sound

# Interactions of Sound Waves

(pages 542–543)

***Key Concept:*** **Sound waves reflect off objects, diffract through narrow openings and around barriers, and interfere with each other.**

- Sound waves can reflect, or bounce back. This happens when sound waves hit a wall or other hard surface. A reflected sound wave is called an **echo**. If you shout in an empty gym, you can hear an echo.

- Sound waves can diffract, or bend and spread out. Sound waves diffract when they pass through openings or around walls. You might hear someone talking around a corner because sound waves can bend and spread out.

- Sound waves can interfere, or bump into one another. When sound waves interfere, they make a single wave.

*Answer the following questions. Use your textbook and the ideas above.*

3. Read the words in the box. In each sentence below, fill in one of the words.

| | | |
|---|---|---|
| interference | echo | diffraction |

  a. A reflected sound wave is called a(an) _____.

  b. When sound waves bump into one another, it is called _____.

4. Circle the letter of the type of sound wave interaction that the picture shows.
   a. reflection
   b. diffraction
   c. interference

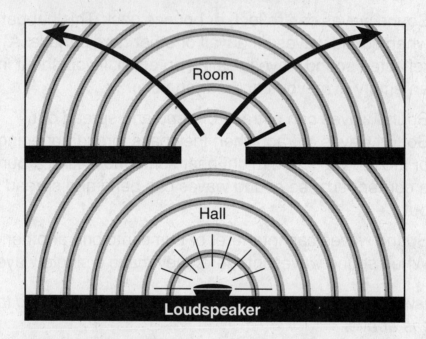

## The Speed of Sound (pages 543–545)

*Key Concept:* **The speed of sound depends on the elasticity, density, and temperature of the medium the sound travels through.**

- Sound travels at different speeds in different mediums. For example, sound usually travels more quickly in solids than in gases.

- Sound travels faster in mediums that are elastic, or stretchy. A rubber band is very stretchy. Therefore, sound travels quickly in a rubber band.

**Sound**

- Sound travels more slowly in denser mediums. Something that is dense feels heavy for its size. Lead is a very dense solid. Therefore, sound travels more slowly in lead than in most other solids.

- Sound travels more quickly when the medium is warm. For example, sound travels more quickly in air that is 20°C than in air that is 0°C.

*Answer the following questions. Use your textbook and the ideas on page 230 and above.*

5. Is the following sentence true or false? Sound travels at the same speed in all mediums. _____

6. Fill in the blank in the concept map about the speed of sound.

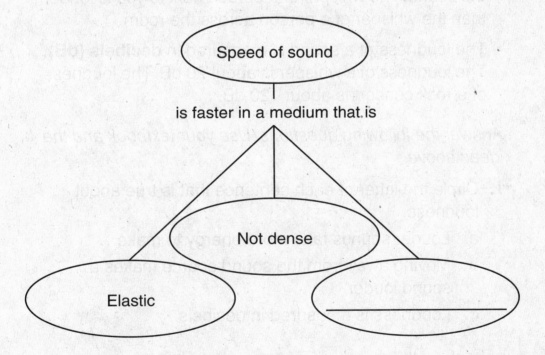

Speed of sound

is faster in a medium that is

Not dense

Elastic

_____

# Properties of Sound (pages 546–551)

## Loudness (pages 546–548)

*Key Concept:* **The loudness of a sound depends on two factors: the amount of energy it takes to make the sound and the distance from the source of the sound.**

- **Loudness** is how loud or soft a sound seems to the person who hears it.

- The more energy it takes to make a sound, the louder the sound. For example, pounding hard on a door with your fist makes a louder sound than tapping gently on a door with your fingers.

- The closer you are to the source of a sound, the louder the sound. The whisper of a person next to you is louder than the whisper of a person across the room.

- The loudness of a sound is measured in **decibels (dB)**. The loudness of a whisper is about 20 dB. The loudness of a rock concert is about 120 dB.

*Answer the following questions. Use your textbook and the ideas above.*

1. Circle the letter of each sentence that is true about loudness.
    a. Louder sounds take more energy to make.
    b. Moving away from the sound source makes a sound louder.
    c. Loudness is measured in decibels.

2. Is the following sentence true or false? Sounds are louder when you are closer to them. _____

## Pitch (pages 548–549)

**Key Concept: The pitch of a sound that you hear depends on the frequency of the sound wave.**

- **Pitch** is how high or low a sound seems to a person who hears it. The sound of a whistle has a high pitch. The sound of thunder has a low pitch.

- The pitch of a sound depends on the frequency of the sound waves. A sound wave with a higher frequency makes a sound with a higher pitch.

- Humans can hear only a certain range of pitches. A sound that is too high for humans to hear is called **ultrasound**. A sound that is too low for humans to hear is called **infrasound**.

- Music uses certain pitches called notes. When you sing or play a musical instrument, you keep changing pitch.

*Answer the following questions. Use your textbook and the ideas above.*

3. How high or low a sound seems to a person who hears it is the _____.

4. Is the following sentence true or false? The pitch of a sound depends on the frequency of the sound waves.

   _____

5. Fill in the blanks in the table about types of sound.

| Types of Sound | |
|---|---|
| a. _____ | too high for humans to hear |
| b. _____ | too low for humans to hear |

# The Doppler Effect (pages 550–551)

*Key Concept:* **When a sound source moves, the frequency of the waves changes because the motion of the source adds to the motion of the waves.**

- The **Doppler effect** is a change in pitch that happens when a sound source is moving. For example, when a fire truck races by you, the sound of the siren changes pitch.

- When a fire truck is coming toward you, the truck is moving in the same direction as the sound waves you are hearing. This makes the waves closer together. The waves have a higher frequency, so the sound has a higher pitch.

- When the fire truck is going away from you, the truck is moving in the opposite direction from the sound waves you are hearing. This makes the waves farther apart. The waves have a lower frequency, so the sound has a lower pitch.

*Answer the following questions. Use your textbook and the ideas above.*

6. Which property of a sound wave changes in the Doppler effect? Circle the letter of the correct answer.
   a. loudness
   b. speed
   c. frequency

**Sound**

7. Both people in the picture hear the fire truck's siren. Which person is hearing a lower pitch? Which person is hearing a higher pitch?

a. _____

b. _____

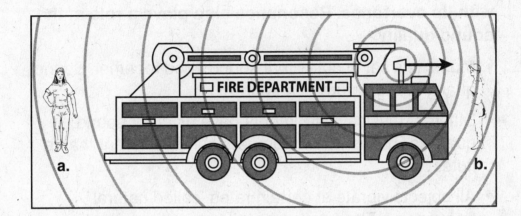

**Sound**

# Music (pages 552–556)

## Sound Quality (page 553)

*Key Concept:* The sound quality of musical instruments results from blending a fundamental tone with its overtones. Resonance also plays a role in the sound quality.

- **Music** is a set of notes that sound good together. Sound quality is the nature of a sound.

- Different musical instruments have different sound qualities. This is why a trumpet sounds different than a flute.

- All objects vibrate at certain rates, called natural frequencies. The **fundamental tone** is the lowest natural frequency of an object. **Overtones** are higher natural frequencies of an object.

- Different musical instruments have different overtones. This gives them different sound qualities.

- Resonance also affects the sound quality of musical instruments. Resonance happens when outside vibrations have the same frequencies as an object's natural frequencies. Resonance makes some overtones louder.

*Answer the following questions. Use your textbook and the ideas above.*

1. A set of notes that sound good together is called

   _____.

2. How does resonance affect sound quality? Circle the letter of the correct answer.

   a. by making the fundamental tone louder

   b. by making the fundamental tone higher

   c. by making some overtones louder

**3.** The picture shows two sound waves with different frequencies. Which sound wave is the fundamental tone? Which sound wave is the overtone?

a. _____

b. _____

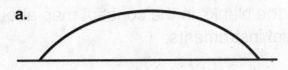

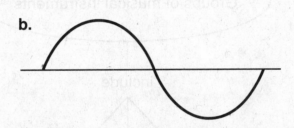

# Groups of Musical Instruments (pages 554–555)

*Key Concept:* **There are three basic groups of musical instruments: stringed instruments, wind instruments, and percussion instruments.**

- In all musical instruments, something vibrates to make sound. Instruments also have ways to change the loudness and pitch of the sound.

- Stringed instruments include guitars and violins. The strings vibrate when players strum them or rub them with a bow.

- Wind instruments include trumpets and clarinets. The players' lips or thin strips of material vibrate when players blow into the instruments.

- Percussion instruments include drums and cymbals. Parts of these instruments vibrate when players hit them with their hands or with sticks.

**Sound**

*Answer the following questions. Use your textbook and the ideas on page 237.*

4. Is the following sentence true or false? In all musical instruments, something vibrates to make sounds.

_____

5. Fill in the blanks in the concept map about groups of musical instruments.

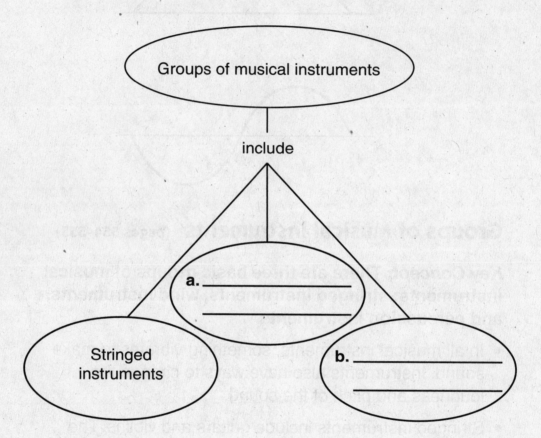

Groups of musical instruments

include

a. _____

_____

Stringed instruments

b. _____

_____

**Sound**

## Acoustics (page 556)

*Key Concept:* **Acoustics is used in the design of concert halls to control reverberation and interference.**

- **Acoustics** is the study of the way sounds bounce off surfaces and bump into one another.

- When sound waves bounce off hard surfaces, echoes form. If the echoes continue after the sound stops, it is called **reverberation**. Reverberation can make it hard to hear sounds clearly.

- When sound waves bump into one another, it is called interference. Interference can make sounds too loud or too soft.

- When people design concert halls, they try to control reverberation and interference. For example, they use soft materials on some of the walls. Fewer sound waves bounce back, so there is less reverberation.

*Answer the following question. Use your textbook and the ideas above.*

6. Read the words in the box. In each sentence below, fill in one of the words.

| | | |
|---|---|---|
| acoustics | vibration | interference |
| reverberation | | |

a. When echoes of a sound continue after the sound stops, it is called _____.

b. When sound waves bump into one another, it is called _____.

c. The study of the way sounds bump into one another and bounce off surfaces is

_____.

# How You Hear Sound (pages 558–560)

## The Human Ear (pages 558–559)

*Key Concept:* **The outer ear funnels sound waves, the middle ear transmits the waves inward, and the inner ear converts sound waves into a form that travels to your brain.**

- The ear is divided into three main sections: the outer ear, the middle ear, and the inner ear.

- The outer ear gathers sound waves. The sound waves travel to a thin sheet called the **eardrum**. The sound waves make the eardrum vibrate. The eardrum passes the vibrations to the middle ear.

- The middle ear contains three tiny bones. The vibrations travel through the three tiny bones to the inner ear.

- The inner ear changes the vibrations into signals. The signals travel to the brain.

*Answer the following questions. Use your textbook and the ideas above.*

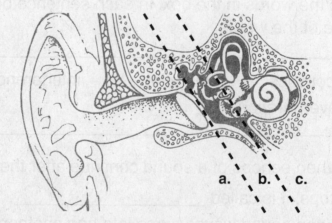

a.    b.    c.

1. The picture shows the three main sections of the ear. Which section, a, b, or c, changes vibrations into signals? _____

2. In which section, a, b, or c, is the eardrum? _____

# Hearing Loss (page 560)

*Key Concept:* **There are many causes of hearing loss, including injury, infection, exposure to loud sounds, and aging.**

- Hearing loss means losing some or all of your hearing. People with hearing loss often cannot hear very soft or high-pitched sounds.

- Aging is the most common cause of hearing loss. Injury and loud sounds are other causes.

- To help protect your ears from injury, never put objects into your ears. To help protect your ears from loud sounds, wear hearing protection such as earplugs.

*Answer the following questions. Use your textbook and the ideas above.*

3. Is the following sentence true or false? All people with hearing loss can no longer hear any sounds.

   _____

4. Which cause of hearing loss can be prevented by wearing hearing protection? Circle the letter of the correct answer.

   a. infection

   b. loud sounds

   c. aging

# Using Sound (pages 564–567)

## Echolocation (page 565)

*Key Concept:* Some animals, including bats and dolphins, use echolocation to navigate and to find food.

- **Echolocation** (ek oh loh KAY shun) is the use of reflected sound waves to find objects in the dark.

- Bats and dolphins use echolocation to move and hunt in the dark. The animals send out ultrasound waves, which bounce off objects. The reflected waves return to the animals and tell them where the objects are.

*Answer the following questions. Use your textbook and the ideas above.*

1. The use of reflected sound waves to find objects in the dark is called _____.

2. The picture shows a dolphin sending out sound waves. The sound waves bounce off a fish. Which sound waves, a or b, tell the dolphin where the fish is?

   _____

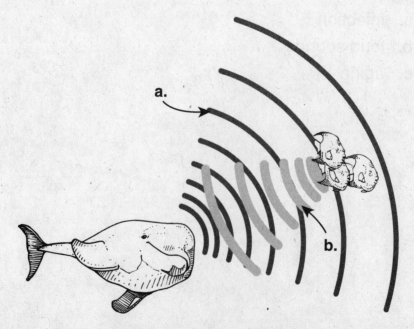

**Sound**

# Ultrasound Technologies (pages 566–567)

*Key Concept:* **Ultrasound technologies such as sonar and ultrasound imaging are used to observe things that cannot be seen directly.**

- **Sonar** uses ultrasound waves to find underwater objects, such as sunken ships.

- A sonar device sends ultrasound waves into the water. The waves bounce off objects and return to the device. The waves take longer to return when the objects are farther away.

- Ultrasound imaging uses ultrasound waves to look inside the human body.

- A device sends ultrasound waves into the body. The waves bounce off body parts and return to the device. The reflected waves are used to make a picture called a **sonogram**.

*Answer the following questions. Use your textbook and the ideas above.*

3. Read the words in the box. In each sentence below, fill in one of the words.

| echolocation    sonar    sonogram |

   a. A picture made from reflected ultrasound waves is a(an) _____.

   b. The use of ultrasound to find objects underwater is _____.

**Sound**

4. Fill in the blank in the table about ultrasound
technologies.

| Ultrasound Technologies | |
|---|---|
| **Type of Technology** | **Use** |
| a. _____ | finding objects underwater |
| b. _____ | looking inside the human body |

**The Electromagnetic Spectrum**

# The Nature of Electromagnetic Waves (pages 574–577)

## What Is an Electromagnetic Wave?
(pages 575–576)

*Key Concept:* **An electromagnetic wave consists of vibrating electric and magnetic fields that move through space at the speed of light.**

- An **electromagnetic wave** is a transverse wave that carries electrical and magnetic energy. The energy is called **electromagnetic radiation**. Light is an example of an electromagnetic wave.

- Electromagnetic waves do not need a medium to travel through. They can travel though empty space. For example, sunlight travels through empty space to reach Earth.

- All electromagnetic waves travel at the same speed. In empty space, they travel at about 300,000 km per second. This speed is called the speed of light.

*Answer the following questions. Use your textbook and the ideas above.*

1. Circle the letter of the type of wave that is an electromagnetic wave.

    a. transverse wave

    b. longitudinal wave

    c. sound wave

2. Is the following sentence true or false? Electromagnetic waves need a medium to travel through. _____

3. The speed of light in empty space is

    _____.

**The Electromagnetic Spectrum**

# Models of Electromagnetic Waves

**(pages 576–577)**

*Key Concept:* **Many properties of electromagnetic waves can be explained by a wave model. However, some properties are best explained by a particle model.**

- Both a wave model and a particle model are needed to explain how light behaves.

- Sometimes light behaves like waves. The waves vibrate in all directions. You can use a special filter to block light waves that vibrate in every direction except one. Only light that vibrates in that one direction passes through the filter. This light is called **polarized light**.

- Sometimes light behaves like a stream of tiny particles of energy. A particle of light energy is called a **photon**. When photons hit a material, they can knock other particles out of the material. When this happens, it is called the **photoelectric effect**.

*Answer the following questions. Use your textbook and the ideas above.*

**4.** Fill in the blanks in the table about models of light.

| Models of Light | |
| --- | --- |
| **Model** | **How Light Behaves** |
| a. _____ model | like waves |
| b. _____ model | like a stream of particles |

Name _____ Date _____ Class _____

**The Electromagnetic Spectrum**

5. Read the words in the box. In each sentence below, fill in one of the words.

> polarized      photon      interference
>
> photoelectric

a. When light knocks particles out of a material, it is called the _____ effect.

b. A particle of light energy is known as a(an) _____.

c. Light that vibrates in just one direction after passing through a special filter is called _____ light.

6. The drawing shows one model of light. Circle the letter of the model it shows.

a. wave model

b. photon model

c. particle model

Direction of wave

# Waves of the Electromagnetic Spectrum (pages 578–585)

## What Is the Electromagnetic Spectrum?
(page 579)

*Key Concept:* **All electromagnetic waves travel at the same speed in a vacuum, but they have different wavelengths and different frequencies. The electromagnetic spectrum is made up of radio waves, infrared rays, visible light, ultraviolet rays, X-rays, and gamma rays.**

- The **electromagnetic spectrum** is the complete range of electromagnetic waves. The waves are placed in order of increasing frequency. As the frequencies of the waves get higher, their wavelengths get shorter.

- At one end of the electromagnetic spectrum are radio waves. Radio waves have low frequencies and long wavelengths. At the other end of the spectrum are gamma rays. Gamma rays have high frequencies and short wavelengths.

- The higher the frequency of electromagnetic waves, the more energy they have. Gamma waves have the highest frequency, so they have the most energy.

*Answer the following question. Use your textbook and the ideas above.*

1. The diagram shows the electromagnetic spectrum. Fill in the missing waves.

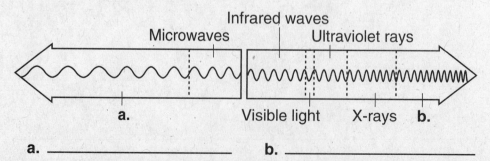

a. _____ b. _____

**The Electromagnetic Spectrum**

## Radio Waves  (page 580)

*Key Concept:* **Radio waves are at one end of the electromagnetic spectrum.**

- **Radio waves** are electromagnetic waves with the lowest frequencies and longest wavelengths.

- Radio waves with the very lowest frequencies are used to carry signals for radio and television programs.

- Radio waves with the highest frequencies are called **microwaves**. Microwaves are used to cook food. Microwaves are also used in radar. **Radar** uses reflected microwaves to detect objects, such as moving cars.

*Answer the following question. Use your textbook and the ideas above.*

2. Circle the letter of each sentence that is true about radio waves.

   **a.** Radio waves have very high frequencies.

   **b.** Radio waves have very long wavelengths.

   **c.** Radio waves include microwaves.

## Infrared Rays  (page 581)

*Key Concept:* **Infrared rays follow radio waves in the electromagnetic spectrum.**

- **Infrared rays** are electromagnetic waves with higher frequencies and shorter wavelengths than radio waves.

- Infrared rays have more energy than radio waves because they have higher frequencies. You can feel the energy of infrared rays as heat. Heat lamps give off infrared rays.

- Most objects give off some infrared rays. You can use an infrared camera to see objects in the dark.

*Answer the following questions. Use your textbook and the ideas on page 249.*

3. Is the following sentence true or false? Infrared rays have lower frequencies than radio waves? _____

4. Circle the letter of a use of infrared rays.
   a. heat lamps
   b. television signals
   c. radar

## Visible Light (page 582)

*Key Concept:* **Visible light follows infrared rays in the electromagnetic spectrum.**

- Electromagnetic waves that you can see are called **visible light**. Visible light has higher frequencies and shorter wavelengths than infrared rays.

- We see different wavelengths of visible light as different colors. From longest to shortest wavelengths, the colors of visible light are red, orange, yellow, green, blue, and violet. Visible light that looks white is really a mixture of all the different colors of light.

*Answer the following question. Use your textbook and the ideas above.*

5. Fill in the blanks in the concept map about visible light.

```
                    ┌──────────────┐
                    │ Visible light │
                    └──────────────┘
                            │
           from longest to shortest wavelengths
                            │
```

| red | orange | a._____ | green | blue | b._____ |
|-----|--------|-------------|-------|------|-------------|

**The Electromagnetic Spectrum**

## Ultraviolet Rays (page 582)

***Key Concept:* Ultraviolet rays follow visible light in the electromagnetic spectrum.**

- **Ultraviolet rays** are electromagnetic waves with higher frequencies and shorter wavelengths than visible light.

- Ultraviolet rays have more energy than visible light because they have higher frequencies.

- Ultraviolet rays help our bodies make vitamin D. However, too many ultraviolet rays can cause sunburn and skin cancer.

*Answer the following question. Use your textbook and the ideas above.*

6. Circle the letter of each sentence that is true about ultraviolet rays.

   a. Ultraviolet rays have higher frequencies than visible light.

   b. Ultraviolet rays have longer wavelengths than visible light.

   c. Ultraviolet rays have less energy than visible light.

## X-Rays (page 583)

***Key Concept:* X-rays follow ultraviolet rays in the electromagnetic spectrum.**

- **X-rays** are electromagnetic waves with higher frequencies and shorter wavelengths than ultraviolet rays.

- X-rays have more energy than ultraviolet rays because they have higher frequencies. X-rays have enough energy to pass through many materials, including skin.

- X-rays are used to take pictures of bones and teeth. Too many X-rays can cause cancer.

**The Electromagnetic Spectrum**

*Answer the following questions. Use your textbook and the ideas on page 251.*

7. Is the following sentence true or false? X-rays have higher frequencies and shorter wavelengths than ultraviolet rays. _____

8. Circle the letter of a use of X-rays.
   a. making vitamin D
   b. taking pictures of bones and teeth
   c. heating food

## Gamma Rays (pages 584–585)

*Key Concept:* **Gamma rays follow X-rays in the electromagnetic spectrum.**

- **Gamma rays** are electromagnetic waves with the highest frequencies and shortest wavelengths.

- Gamma rays have more energy than any other type of electromagnetic wave. Gamma rays have enough energy to pass through most materials.

- Gamma rays can be used to kill cancer cells inside the body.

- Some objects in space give off gamma rays. Special telescopes can detect these gamma rays.

*Answer the following questions. Use your textbook and the ideas above.*

9. The electromagnetic waves with the highest frequencies and shortest wavelengths are

   _____.

10. Is the following sentence true or false? Gamma rays have more energy than X-rays. _____

Name _____ Date _____ Class _____

# Producing Visible Light (pages 588–591)

## Incandescent Lights (pages 588–589)

*Key Concept:* **Incandescent lights are one common type of light bulb.**

- An **incandescent light** is a light bulb that glows when a thin wire inside it gets very hot. The thin wire is called a filament. The filament is made of the metal tungsten. The filament glows with white light when electricity passes through it.

- There are two types of incandescent light bulbs: ordinary light bulbs and tungsten-halogen light bulbs. The two types of bulbs contain different gases. Tungsten-halogen bulbs give off more light and use less energy than ordinary light bulbs.

*Answer the following questions. Use your textbook and the ideas above.*

1. The picture shows an ordinary incandescent light bulb. Circle the letter of the part that gives off light.

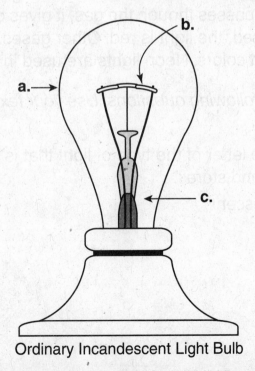

Ordinary Incandescent Light Bulb

**The Electromagnetic Spectrum**

**2.** Is the following sentence true or false? Tungsten-halogen light bulbs use more energy than ordinary light bulbs. _____

## Other Light Sources (pages 590–591)

*Key Concept:* **Fluorescent lights, vapor lights, and neon lights are other common types of light bulbs.**

- A **fluorescent** (floo RES unt) **light** contains a gas and a powder. When electricity passes through the gas, it gives off ultraviolet rays. The ultraviolet rays cause the powder to give off light. Fluorescent lights give off more light and use less energy than incandescent lights. Fluorescent lights are used in schools and stores.

- A **vapor light** contains a gas and a small amount of solid sodium or mercury. When electricity passes through the gas, it heats up and changes the sodium or mercury to a glowing gas. Vapor lights give off a lot of light and use very little energy. Vapor lights are used to light streets and parking lots.

- A **neon light** contains neon or another gas. When electricity passes though the gas, it gives off light. When neon is used, the light is red. Other gases give off light of different colors. Neon lights are used in signs.

*Answer the following questions. Use your textbook and the ideas above.*

**3.** Circle the letter of the type of light that is used inside schools and stores.
   **a.** fluorescent
   **b.** vapor
   **c.** neon

**The Electromagnetic Spectrum**

4. Is the following sentence true or false? Neon lights are used to light streets and parking lots. _____

5. Fill in the blanks in the table comparing types of lights.

| Types of Lights | |
|---|---|
| **Type of Light** | **Material That Gives off Light** |
| Fluorescent light | a powder |
| **a.** _____ light | sodium or mercury |
| **b.** _____ light | neon or other gas |

# Wireless Communication

(pages 594–600)

## Radio and Television (pages 594–596)

*Key Concept:* **Transmission antennas send out, or broadcast, radio waves in all directions. Radio waves carry information from the antenna of a broadcasting station to the receiving antenna of your radio or television.**

- Radio waves carry signals for both radio and television programs. There are two ways to send signals: amplitude modulation and frequency modulation.

- In **amplitude modulation** (AM), signals are sent by constantly changing the amplitude of the radio wave. (Remember, the amplitude of a transverse wave is how far the medium moves up or down.) Amplitude modulation is used by AM radio stations and by television stations for pictures.

- In **frequency modulation** (FM), signals are sent by constantly changing the frequency of the radio wave. (Remember, the frequency of a wave is how many waves pass a point in a given amount of time.) Frequency modulation is used by FM radio stations and by television stations for sound.

- Radio waves also carry signals for other kinds of radios, such as police radios.

*Answer the following questions. Use your textbook and the ideas above.*

**1.** Is the following sentence true or false? Radio waves carry signals for both radio and television programs.

_____

**The Electromagnetic Spectrum**

2. The picture shows two different radio waves. Which wave shows amplitude modulation? Which wave shows frequency modulation?

   a. _____

   b. _____

a.

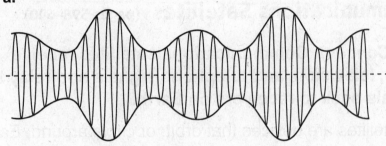

b.

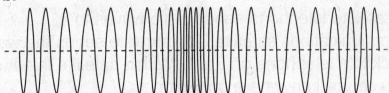

## Cellular Phones (page 597)

***Key Concept:* Cellular phones transmit and receive signals using high-frequency microwaves.**

- When you place a call on a cellular phone, the phone sends out microwaves. (Remember, microwaves are radio waves with the highest frequencies.)

- A cellular phone tower picks up the microwaves and sends them to a central hub. The central hub sends the microwaves to another tower or cellular phone.

*Answer the following questions. Use your textbook and the ideas above.*

3. Is the following sentence true or false? A cellular phone sends waves directly to another phone. _____

**4.** Circle the letter of the type of radio wave that is used by cellular phones.

   **a.** microwave

   **b.** FM wave

   **c.** AM wave

## Communications Satellites (pages 598–600)

*Key Concept:* **Communications satellites receive radio, television, and telephone signals and relay the signals back to receivers on Earth.**

- Satellites are devices that orbit, or circle around, Earth. Communications satellites receive radio waves and send them back to Earth. The satellites are used for radio, television, and telephone signals.

- A satellite telephone sends radio waves to a communications satellite. The satellite sends the waves back to a telephone on Earth. With a satellite telephone, you can call anywhere on Earth.

- Radio and television stations also send radio waves to communications satellites. The satellites send the waves to local stations around the world. Many people have their own satellite dishes. The dishes let people receive the waves directly from the satellite.

- The Global Positioning System (GPS) uses many satellites that send radio signals to Earth. Anyone with a GPS receiver can pick up the signals. The signals tell you exactly where you are. GPS receivers are found in airplanes, boats, and cars.

*Answer the following questions. Use your textbook and the ideas above.*

**5.** Is the following sentence true or false? Communications satellites are used only for telephone signals. _____

**The Electromagnetic Spectrum**

6. What type of electromagnetic wave does a communications satellite receive and send? Circle the letter of the correct answer.
   a. radio wave
   b. ultraviolet wave
   c. gamma ray

7. What is the Global Positioning System used for? Circle the letter of the correct answer.
   a. receiving television programs
   b. making telephone calls
   c. finding out where you are

# Light and Color (pages 610–615)

## When Light Strikes an Object (page 611)

*Key Concept:* **When light strikes an object, the light can be reflected, transmitted, or absorbed.**

- Materials can be transparent, translucent, or opaque. It depends on what happens to the light that hits the materials.

- **Transparent materials** let most light pass right through. You can see clearly through a transparent material. Clear glass is a transparent material.

- **Translucent** (trans LOO sunt) **materials** scatter light as it passes through. You can see things through a translucent material, but the details are blurred. Wax paper is a translucent material.

- **Opaque** (oh PAYK) **materials** do not let light pass through. They reflect or absorb all the light that hits them. When materials absorb light, they take in light. You cannot see anything through an opaque material. Wood is an opaque material.

*Answer the following questions. Use your textbook and the ideas above.*

1. Is the following sentence true or false? Wax paper is a transparent material. _____

2. Circle the letter of the type of material that a blackboard is.
   a. transparent
   b. translucent
   c. opaque

**3.** Fill in the blanks in the table about types of materials and light.

| Types of Materials and Light | |
|---|---|
| **Type of Material** | **What Happens to Light That Hits It** |
| Transparent | light passes right through |
| a. _____ | light is scattered as it passes through |
| b. _____ | light is reflected or absorbed |

## The Color of Objects (pages 612–613)

**Key Concept: The color of an opaque object is the color of the light it reflects. The color of a transparent or translucent object is the color of the light it transmits.**

- The color of any object depends on what the object is made of and the color of light that hits it.

- Objects made of opaque materials reflect some light and absorb the rest. The color of the reflected light gives an opaque object its color. For example, an apple looks red because it reflects red light and absorbs light of other colors.

- Objects made of transparent or translucent materials transmit, or let through, only certain colors of light. The color of light that passes through a transparent or translucent object gives the object its color. For example, if sunglasses let only green light pass through, the glasses look green.

*Answer the following questions. Use your textbook and the ideas on page 261.*

**4.** Is the following sentence true or false? The color of an object depends on what the object is made of and what color of light hits it. _____

**5.** Fill in the blanks in the concept map about the color of objects.

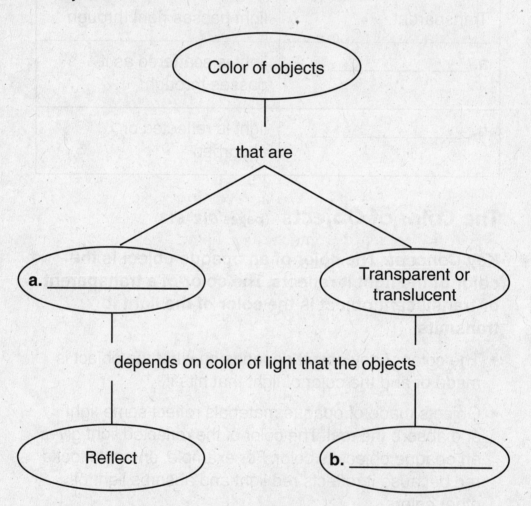

**6.** If a ball reflects red light and absorbs light of other colors, what color does the ball appear? Circle the letter of the correct answer.

    **a.** red

    **b.** green

    **c.** black

**Light**

## Combining Colors (pages 614–615)

*Key Concept:* **When combined in equal amounts, the three primary colors of light produce white light. As pigments are added together, fewer colors of light are reflected and more are absorbed.**

- **Primary colors** are three colors that can mix together to make any other color. Two primary colors mix in equal amounts to make a **secondary color**.

- Primary colors of light are red, green, and blue. Secondary colors of light are yellow (red and green), cyan (blue and green), and magenta (blue and red). Equal amounts of all three primary colors of light mix together to make white light.

- **Pigments** are colored materials. They are used to color inks and paints. Pigments have different primary and secondary colors than light.

- Primary colors of pigments are yellow, cyan, and magenta. Secondary colors of pigments are red (yellow and magenta), green (yellow and cyan), and blue (cyan and magenta). When equal amounts of all three primary pigment colors are mixed together, the mixture looks black.

*Answer the following questions. Use your textbook and the ideas above.*

7. What do you get when you mix equal amounts of all three primary colors of light? Circle the letter of the correct answer.

    a. yellow light

    b. cyan light

    c. white light

8. Fill in the blanks in the table comparing colors of light and pigments.

| Colors of Light and Pigments | | |
|---|---|---|
| **Type of Colors** | **Light** | **Pigments** |
| Primary | red, green, blue | yellow, cyan, magenta |
| Secondary | a. _____ _____ | b. _____ _____ |

9. What do you get when you mix equal amounts of all three primary colors of pigments? Circle the letter of the correct answer.
   a. black pigment
   b. red pigment
   c. blue pigment

**Light**

# Reflection and Mirrors (pages 617–622)

## Reflection of Light Rays (page 618)

*Key Concept:* **The two ways in which a surface can reflect light are regular reflection and diffuse reflection.**

- You can think of light waves as straight lines called **rays**. Light rays can reflect, or bounce off, mirrors and other shiny surfaces.

- When light rays bounce off a smooth surface, it is called **regular reflection**. All the light rays are reflected at the same angle. The reflection is sharp.

- When light rays bounce off a bumpy surface, it is called **diffuse reflection**. The light rays are reflected at different angles. The reflection is blurred.

*Answer the following question. Use your textbook and the ideas above.*

1. The diagrams show light rays being reflected from two different surfaces. Which diagram shows regular reflection? Which diagram shows diffuse reflection?

   a. _____

   b. _____

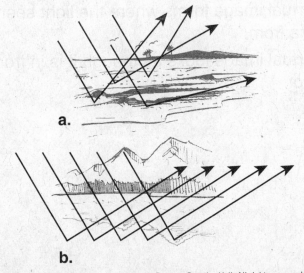

a. _____

b.

**Light**

# Plane Mirrors (page 619)

***Key Concept:*** **A plane mirror produces a virtual image that is upright and the same size as the object.**

- A **plane mirror** is a flat sheet of glass that has a smooth, dark coating on the back. The coating reflects all the light that hits it. Most bathroom mirrors are plane mirrors.

- What you see when you look in a mirror is an image. An **image** is a copy of an object.

- The image you see in a plane mirror is called a virtual image. A **virtual image** is an image that forms where the light seems to come from. The image looks as though it is behind the mirror. A virtual image is always upright, or right side up.

*Answer the following questions. Use your textbook and the ideas above.*

2. Is the following sentence true or false? A plane mirror is a curved sheet of glass that has a smooth, dark coating on the back. _____

3. Circle the letter of each sentence that is true about a virtual image.
    a. A virtual image is always upright.
    b. A virtual image forms where the light seems to come from.
    c. A virtual image looks as though it is in front of a mirror.

**Light**

## Concave Mirrors (pages 620–621)

***Key Concept:* Concave mirrors can form either virtual images or real images.**

- A **concave mirror** is a mirror that curves inward like the inside of a bowl. A concave mirror reflects light rays toward the center of the mirror. The light rays all meet at the same point, called the **focal point**.

- The image formed by a concave mirror is either a virtual image or a real image. The type of image depends on where the object is placed.

- A concave mirror forms a virtual image if the object is between the mirror and the focal point. (Remember, a virtual image is an upright image that seems to form behind the mirror.)

- A concave mirror forms a real image if the object is farther from the mirror than the focal point. A **real image** forms when reflected light rays actually meet. A real image forms in front of the mirror. A real image is always upside down.

*Answer the following questions. Use your textbook and the ideas above.*

4. Is the following sentence true or false? A concave mirror reflects light rays so they all meet at the focal point. _____

**5.** The picture shows an object in front of a concave mirror. Compare the position of the object with the position of the focal point. With the object in this position, will the image be a real image or a virtual image? _____

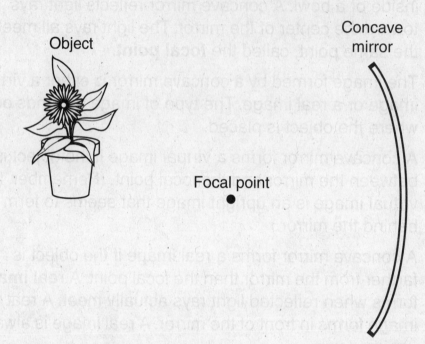

Object

Concave mirror

Focal point

## Convex Mirrors (page 622)

*Key Concept:* **Because the rays never meet, images formed by convex mirrors are always virtual and smaller than the object.**

- A **convex mirror** is a mirror with a surface that curves outward like the outside of a bowl. A convex mirror reflects light rays outward. The reflected rays spread out and never meet. However, the rays seem to be coming from a point behind the mirror. The image looks as though it is behind the mirror.

- Convex mirrors are used in cars as side mirrors. Convex mirrors let you see a bigger area than other mirrors do. Convex mirrors also make objects seem farther away than they really are.

*Answer the following questions. Use your textbook and the ideas on page 268.*

6. A mirror with a surface that curves outward like the outside of a bowl is a(an) _____ mirror.

7. The pictures show an object in front of a convex mirror. Which picture correctly shows how the image should look?_____

**a.**

Object          Convex mirror        Image

**b.**

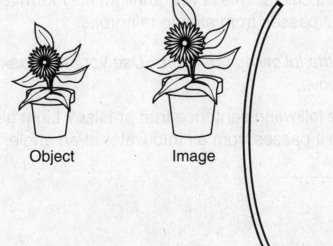

Object          Image          Convex mirror

# Refraction and Lenses (pages 623–627)

## Refraction of Light (pages 624–625)

*Key Concept:* **When light rays enter a medium at an angle, the change in speed causes the rays to bend, or change direction.**

- Light travels at different speeds in different mediums. For example, light travels more slowly in water than in air. Therefore, light slows down when it passes from air into water.

- When light passes from air into water at an angle, one side of the light rays slows down before the other side. This causes the light to bend, or refract.

- How much a medium causes light to slow down and bend is the medium's **index of refraction**. Air has an index of refraction of 1.00. Water has an index of refraction of 1.33. The higher the index of refraction, the more light slows down and bends.

- Remember, white light is made up of light of different colors. Different colors of light have different wavelengths. When light enters a medium at an angle, longer wavelengths of light slow down and bend less than shorter wavelengths. The light separates into different colors. This is why sunlight may form a rainbow when it passes from air into raindrops.

*Answer the following questions. Use your textbook and the ideas above.*

1. Is the following sentence true or false? Light bends when it passes from air into water at an angle.

   _____

**Light**

2. When sunlight passes from air into raindrops, it may

form a _____.

    **a.** medium.

    **b.** refraction.

    **c.** rainbow.

## Lenses (pages 626–627)

*Key Concept:* **An object's position relative to the focal point determines whether a convex lens forms a real image or a virtual image. A concave lens can produce only virtual images because parallel light rays passing through the lens never meet.**

- A **lens** is a curved piece of glass that is used to bend light.

- A lens forms a virtual image or a real image. The type of image depends on the shape of the lens and the position of the object.

- A **convex lens** is thicker in the center than at the edges. A convex lens bends light rays toward the center of the lens. All the rays pass through the focal point.

- The image formed with a convex lens can be a real image or a virtual image. If the object is farther from the lens than the focal point, a real image forms. If the object is closer to the lens than the focal point, a virtual image forms.

- A **concave lens** is thinner in the center than at the edges. A concave lens bends light away from the center of the lens. The light rays never meet, so the image is always a virtual image. The image is upright and smaller than the object.

**Light**

*Answer the following questions. Use your textbook and the ideas on page 271.*

3. The type of lens that is thicker in the center than at the edges is a(an) _____ lens.

4. Is the following sentence true or false? A convex lens can form only virtual images. _____

5. The picture shows an object and its image in front of a concave lens. Is the image a real image or a virtual image?_____

Object

Image

Concave
lens

# Seeing Light (pages 629–632)

## The Human Eye (pages 630–631)

*Key Concept:* **You see objects when a process occurs that involves both your eyes and your brain.**

- Your eyes let you sense light. Your eyes have many parts.

- The **cornea** (KAWR nee uh) is the outside front layer of your eye. It is transparent, so it lets light through. The cornea protects the eye.

- The **pupil** is the part of the eye that looks black. It lets light pass into the eye. The **iris** is the colored part of the eye. It controls the size of the pupil and how much light enters the eye.

- From the pupil, light passes through the lens. The lens is convex. It bends the light to form an image. The image forms on the retina. The **retina** is the inside lining at the back of the eye. The retina sends signals about the image to your brain.

- Your brain makes sense of the signals from the retina. Your brain tells you what you are seeing.

*Answer the following questions. Use your textbook and the ideas above.*

1. Circle the letter of the part of the eye that bends light to form an image.
   a. pupil
   b. iris
   c. lens

2. Is the following sentence true or false? The iris controls the size of the lens. _____

**3.** Fill in the blanks in the flowchart.

**How Light Passes Through the Eye**

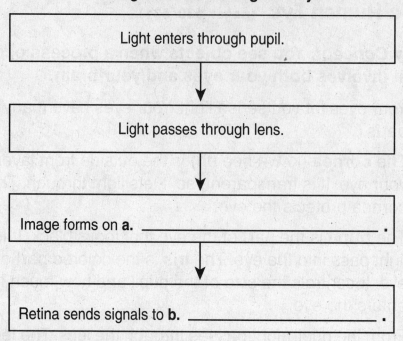

Light enters through pupil.

↓

Light passes through lens.

↓

Image forms on **a.** _____.

↓

Retina sends signals to **b.** _____.

## Correcting Vision (page 632)

*Key Concept:* **Concave lenses are used to correct nearsightedness. Convex lenses are used to correct farsightedness.**

- When an eyeball is too short or too long, images do not form on the retina. This makes the images look blurred. Lenses in glasses or contacts can correct the problem. Lenses focus the images on the retina.

- A **nearsighted** person can see nearby objects clearly, but distant objects look blurred. The eyeball is too long. Images focus in front of the retina. Concave lenses can correct this type of vision problem.

- A **farsighted** person can see distant objects clearly, but nearby objects look blurred. The eyeball is too short. Images focus behind the retina. Convex lenses can correct this type of vision problem.

**Light**

*Answer the following questions. Use your textbook and the ideas on page 274.*

4. The pictures show two different eyes. Which eye belongs to a nearsighted person? Which eye belongs to a farsighted person?

   a. _____

   b. _____

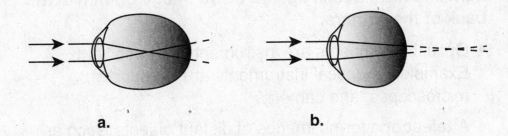

   a.                          b.

5. Is the following sentence true or false? Concave lenses can correct the vision of a farsighted person.

   _____

**Light**

# Using Light (pages 633–641)

## Optical Instruments (pages 634–635)

*Key Concept:* Telescopes use lenses or mirrors to collect and focus light from distant objects. A microscope uses a combination of lenses to produce and magnify an image. A camera uses a lens to focus light and form a real, upside-down image on film in the back of the camera.

- Optical instruments are instruments that use light. Examples of optical instruments are telescopes, microscopes, and cameras.

- A **telescope** forms images of distant objects, such as stars. A telescope makes distant objects look bigger.

- There are two main types of telescopes: refracting and reflecting. A **refracting telescope** uses two lenses to focus light. A **reflecting telescope** uses a lens and a mirror to focus light.

- A **microscope** forms images of small nearby objects, such as germs. A microscope makes small objects look bigger. A microscope uses lenses to focus light.

- A **camera** forms images of objects on film. The film records the images as pictures. A camera uses one or more lenses to focus light.

*Answer the following questions. Use your textbook and the ideas above.*

1. An instrument that uses light is called a(an)

   _____ instrument.

2. A telescope that contains a mirror is a(an)

   _____ telescope.

3. Fill in the blanks in the table about uses of optical instruments.

| Optical Instruments | |
|---|---|
| **Type of Instrument** | **Use** |
| Telescope | makes distant objects look bigger |
| a. _____ | makes small objects look bigger |
| b. _____ | makes pictures of objects |

## Lasers (page 636)

*Key Concept:* **Laser light consists of light waves that all have the same wavelength, or color. The waves are coherent, or in step.**

- A **laser** is a device that produces a special kind of light, called laser light. Laser light has just one wavelength. This makes the light only one color. Also, the waves of laser light are all in step. This means that all the waves overlap one another perfectly.

- A laser is a tube with gases inside. When electricity passes through the tube, the gases give off photons. The photons move around and bump into gas particles. This causes the gases to give off more photons. All the photons move together in a stream. A stream of moving photons is a beam of laser light.

*Answer the following questions. Use your textbook and the ideas above.*

4. A device that produces laser light is called a(an)

_____.

**Light**

5. Is the following sentence true or false? Laser light has just one wavelength. _____

6. Circle the letter of what gives off photons in a laser.
   a. a tube
   b. gases
   c. electricity

## Uses of Lasers (pages 637–639)

*Key Concept:* **In addition to their use by stores, industry, and engineers, lasers are used to read information on compact discs, create holograms, and perform surgery.**

- Lasers have many uses. Stores use lasers to read bar codes. Lasers can be used in industry to cut through metal. Lasers can be used by engineers to make sure things are level.

- Lasers can be used to store and read information on compact discs. When you store information on a compact disk, a laser beam cuts tiny holes in the surface of the disk. When you play the compact disk, a laser beam reads the pattern of holes in the disk.

- Lasers can be used to make holograms. A **hologram** is picture made by laser light. When you walk by a hologram, the picture seems to move.

- Lasers can be used to do surgery. Doctors use lasers to cut through skin and other parts of the body. For example, doctors can use lasers to change the shape of the eye. This can help correct vision problems.

**Light**

*Answer the following questions. Use your textbook and the ideas on page 278.*

**7.** Is the following sentence true or false? Lasers have few uses. _____

**8.** Circle the letter of the description of a hologram.
   **a.** a special type of barcode
   **b.** a picture made by laser light
   **c.** a compact disk read by a laser beam

**9.** Is the following sentence true or false? Lasers can be used to do surgery. _____

## Optical Fibers (pages 640–641)

*Key Concept:* **Optical fibers can carry a laser beam for long distances because the beam stays totally inside the fiber as it travels.**

- Laser beams can be used like radio waves to carry signals. But, laser beams are not sent through the air. Laser beams are sent through optical fibers.

- **Optical fibers** are long, thin strands of glass or plastic. The fibers can carry light for long distances without letting the light escape.

- Optical fibers are used by doctors. They let doctors see inside the body.

- Optical fibers are used to carry signals for telephone calls and television programs. Signals travel more quickly through optical fibers than through wires.

**Light**

*Answer the following questions. Use your textbook and the ideas on page 279.*

**10.** Circle the letter of each sentence that is true about optical fibers.

   **a.** Optical fibers are used to carry laser beams.

   **b.** A lot of light escapes from optical fibers.

   **c.** Signals travel more quickly through optical fibers than through wires.

**11.** Is the following sentence true or false? Doctors use optical fibers to see inside the body. _____

**12.** Complete the concept map about using light.

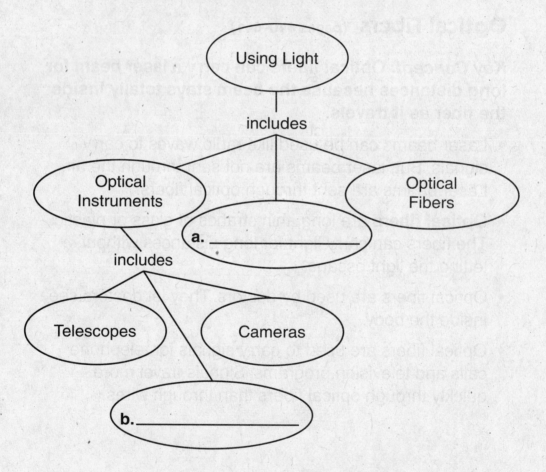

# What Is Magnetism? (pages 654–659)

## Properties of Magnets (page 655)

*Key Concept:* **Magnets attract iron and materials that contain iron. Magnets attract or repel other magnets. In addition, one part of a magnet will always point north when allowed to swing freely.**

- A **magnet** is any material that attracts iron. A magnet also attracts materials that contain iron. A nail, for example, is not all iron. But a nail contains iron.

- Rocks that contain a mineral called magnetite attract iron. Magnetic rocks are known as lodestones.

- If you tie any magnet to a string and then let it hang freely, one part of the magnet will point to the north.

*Answer the following questions. Use your textbook and the ideas above.*

1. A material that attracts iron is called

   a(an) _____.

2. Circle the letter of each sentence that is true about magnets.

   a. Magnets attract or repel other magnets.

   b. Magnetic rocks are called lodestones.

   c. Magnets only attract materials that are all iron.

3. Circle the letter of the direction that one part of a magnet on a string will point.

   a. north

   b. south

   c. east

**Magnetism**

# Magnetic Poles (page 656)

*Key Concept:* **Magnetic poles that are unlike attract each other, and magnetic poles that are alike repel each other.**

- A magnet has two ends. Each end of a magnet is called a **magnetic pole**. The pole that points north is the north pole. The other pole is the south pole.

- The north pole of one magnet and the south pole of another magnet are unlike poles. If you bring unlike poles of two magnets together, the unlike poles will attract, or pull toward, each other.

- The north pole of one magnet and the north pole of another magnet are like poles. If you bring like poles of two magnets together, the like poles will repel, or push away from, each other.

- A force is a push or pull. **Magnetic force** is the attraction (pull) or repulsion (push) between magnetic poles.

*Answer the following questions. Use your textbook and the ideas above.*

4. Draw a line from each term to its meaning.

| Term | Meaning |
|------|---------|
| magnetic pole | **a.** the attraction or repulsion between magnetic poles |
| magnetic force | **b.** the end of a magnet |

5. Is the following sentence true or false? Magnetic poles that are alike attract each other. _____

**Magnetism**

# Magnetic Fields (pages 657–659)

***Key Concept:* Magnetic field lines spread out from one pole, curve around the magnet, and return to the other pole.**

- The area of magnetic force around a magnet is called a **magnetic field**. Magnetic fields cause magnets to attract and repel each other without touching.

- You can map out the magnetic field around a magnet with magnetic field lines. Magnetic field lines are imaginary lines used to show a magnetic field.

- Magnetic field lines loop from the north pole to the south pole. They never overlap. Where the lines are closest, the magnetic field is strongest.

- When the magnetic fields of two or more magnets overlap, the result is called a combined magnetic field.

*Answer the following questions. Use your textbook and the ideas above.*

**6.** The area of force around a magnet is called a

  magnetic _____.

**7.** Circle the letter of each sentence that is true about magnetic fields.

   **a.** Magnets have to touch for the magnetic fields of the magnets to interact.

   **b.** Magnetic fields can cause magnets to attract each other without touching.

   **c.** When magnetic fields of magnets overlap, the result is called a combined magnetic field.

**Magnetism**

8. The picture below shows a magnet with half of a
   magnetic field. Use magnetic field lines to draw the
   other half of the magnetic field around the magnet.

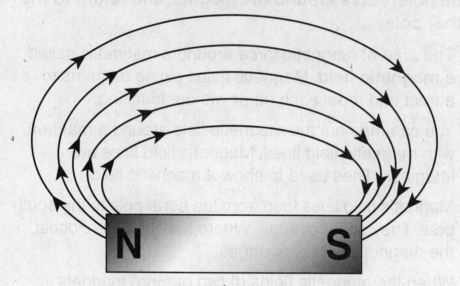

**Magnetism**

# Inside a Magnet (pages 662–667)

## The Atom (page 663)

*Key Concept:* **A spinning electron produces a magnetic field that makes the electron behave like a tiny magnet in an atom.**

- An **element** is one of the basic materials that makes up matter. An **atom** is the smallest particle of an element that still has the properties of the element.

- An atom has a center region called a **nucleus**. The nucleus contains two kinds of particles: protons and neutrons. Electrons are around the nucleus. An **electron** is a particle that has a negative charge.

- Each electron has a property called electron spin. An electron acts like it is spinning. The spinning of an electron produces a magnetic field. An electron is like a tiny magnet inside an atom.

*Answer the following questions. Use your textbook and the ideas above.*

1. Circle the letter of each sentence that is true about electrons.
    a. Each electron has a property called electron spin.
    b. Electrons are particles that exist inside the nucleus of an atom.
    c. The spinning of an electron produces a magnetic field.

2. Is the following sentence true or false? A nucleus contains electrons and protons. _____

**Magnetism**

3. Read each word in the box. In each sentence below, fill in one of the words.

| atom | nucleus | electron | element | proton |
|------|---------|----------|---------|--------|

a. The smallest particle of an element that still has the properties of the element is a(an)

_____.

b. A(an) _____ is like a tiny magnet inside an atom.

c. An atom has a center region called a(an)

_____.

d. One of the basic materials that makes up matter

is a(an) _____.

## Magnetic Domains (pages 664–665)

*Key Concept:* **In a magnetized material, all or most of the magnetic domains are arranged in the same direction.**

- In some materials, the magnetic fields of many atoms point in the same direction. A **magnetic domain** is a group of atoms that have their magnetic fields all pointing in the same direction.

- A magnetic domain acts like a bar magnet. A magnetic domain has a north pole and a south pole.

- A material that is magnetized has all or most of its magnetic domains pointing in the same direction. The magnetic fields of the domains are lined up.

- A material that has strong magnetic properties is called a **ferromagnetic material**. In nature, ferromagnetic materials include iron and nickel. Most magnets are made of a ferromagnetic material called ferrite.

**Magnetism**

*Answer the following questions. Use your textbook and the ideas on page 286.*

**4.** Draw a line from each term to its meaning.

| **Term** | **Meaning** |
|---|---|
| magnetic domain | **a.** a material that has strong magnetic properties |
| ferromagnetic material | **b.** a group of atoms that have their magnetic fields all pointing in the same direction |

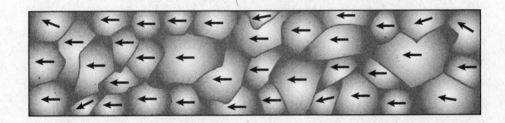

**5.** The picture above shows the insides of a magnetized material. Circle the letter of the sentence that is true about this material.

**a.** Most of the magnetic domains point in all different directions.

**b.** Most of the magnetic domains point in the same direction.

**c.** The material has no magnetic domains.

# Making and Changing Magnets (pages 666–667)

*Key Concept:* **Magnets can be made, destroyed, or broken apart.**

- When you magnetize a material, you make a magnet. For example, when you rub a steel paper clip against a magnet, the paper clip becomes a magnet.

- A magnet made from a material that easily loses its magnetism is called a **temporary magnet**. A magnet made from a material that keeps its magnetism for a long time is called a **permanent magnet**.

- You can destroy a magnet in two main ways: by hitting it hard or by heating it.

- When you break apart a magnet, each smaller piece has a north pole and a south pole.

*Answer the following questions. Use your textbook and the ideas above.*

**6.** Complete the table about magnets.

| Types of Magnets | |
|---|---|
| **Type of Magnet** | **Description** |
| **a.** _____ magnet | a magnet made from a material that easily loses its magnetism |
| **b.** _____ magnet | a magnet made from a material that keeps its magnetism for a long time |

**7.** Is the following sentence true or false? When you break apart a magnet, the small pieces have only north poles. _____

**Magnetism**

# Magnetic Earth (pages 670–675)

## Earth as a Magnet (pages 671–672)

*Key Concept:* **Just like a bar magnet, Earth has a magnetic field surrounding it and two magnetic poles.**

- Earth has a magnetic field. Earth's magnetic field makes a compass needle point north. A **compass** has a magnetized needle that spins around freely.

- Earth has magnetic poles. A magnetic pole is the place at the top or bottom of Earth where the magnetic field is strongest.

- Earth's magnetic poles are not at the same places as Earth's geographic North and South poles. The geographic poles are at the ends of Earth's axis.

*Answer the following questions. Use your textbook and the ideas above.*

1. Draw a line from each term to its meaning.

   **Term**

   compass

   magnetic pole

   **Meaning**

   **a.** a device that has a magnetized needle that spins around freely

   **b.** the place at the top or bottom of Earth where the magnetic field is strongest

2. Is the following sentence true or false? Earth's geographic North Pole is at the same place as Earth's magnetic north pole. _____

**Magnetism**

# Earth's Magnetic Field (pages 672–673)

***Key Concept:*** **Since Earth produces a strong magnetic field, Earth itself can make magnets out of ferromagnetic materials.**

- Earth's magnetic field can make some objects into magnets. For example, if you leave an iron bar lying in a north-south direction for many years, it will become a magnet.

- Earth's magnetic field also acts on melted rocks that contain iron. The magnetic field makes the iron point north.

- Scientists study the iron in rock at the bottom of the sea. The direction the iron points shows that the positions of Earth's magnetic poles change over time.

*Answer the following questions. Use your textbook and the ideas above.*

**3.** Is the following sentence true or false? Earth's magnetic field can make some objects into magnets.

_____

**4.** Circle the letter of each sentence that is true about Earth's magnetic field.

    **a.** Earth's magnetic field affects iron in rocks.

    **b.** Earth's magnetic poles have always been in the same place.

    **c.** The positions of Earth's magnetic poles change over time.

# The Magnetosphere (pages 674–675)

***Key Concept:*** **Earth's magnetic field affects the movement of electrically charged particles in space.**

- The **Van Allen belts** are regions 1,000 to 25,000 kilometers above Earth on opposite sides of Earth. The Van Allen belts are shaped like doughnuts. The Van Allen belts contain electrons and protons.

- The stream of electrically charged particles from the sun is called **solar wind**. The solar wind pushes on Earth's magnetic field.

- The region of Earth's magnetic field that is shaped by solar wind is called the **magnetosphere**. Solar wind reshapes the magnetosphere as Earth turns on its axis.

- The electrically charged particles from the sun cause a glowing in Earth's atmosphere. An **aurora** is a glowing region of the atmosphere. In the Northern Hemisphere, an aurora is called the Northern Lights.

*Answer the following questions. Use your textbook and the ideas above.*

5. Circle the letter of each sentence that is true about the magnetosphere.

   a. The magnetosphere is shaped like two doughnuts.

   b. Solar wind reshapes the magnetosphere as Earth turns on its axis.

   c. The magnetosphere is part of Earth's magnetic field.

6. Is the following sentence true or false? Electrically charged particles from the sun cause a glowing in Earth's atmosphere. _____

**Magnetism**

7. Complete the table about the magnetosphere.

| The Magnetosphere | |
|---|---|
| **Term** | **Description** |
| Van Allen belts | regions above Earth shaped like<br>a. _____ |
| b. _____ | the stream of electrically charged particles from the sun |
| c. _____ | region of Earth's magnetic field that is shaped by solar wind |
| Aurora | a glowing region called the<br>d. _____<br>in the Northern Hemisphere |

# Electric Charge and Static Electricity (pages 682–689)

## Electric Charge (page 683)

*Key Concept:* **Charges that are the same repel each other. Charges that are different attract each other.**

- Electric charge is a property of protons and electrons. Protons have a positive charge. Electrons have a negative charge.

- Two charges that are the same push away from each other. Two charges that are different pull toward each other.

- If a proton and an electron come close together, they attract each other.

- Attraction (pull) and repulsion (push) between electric charges is known as interaction between charges. The interaction between charges is called electricity.

*Answer the following questions. Use your textbook and the ideas above.*

1. Circle the letter of each sentence that is true about electric charge.
   a. Two charges that are different pull toward each other.
   b. Electrons have a negative charge.
   c. If a proton and an electron come close together, they repel each other.

2. The interaction between charges is called

   _____.

**Electricity**

## Electric Force (page 684)

*Key Concept:* **An electric field is a region around a charged object where the object's electric force is exerted on other charged objects.**

- **Electric force** is the attraction or repulsion between electric charges.

- A magnetic field surrounds a charged object. An **electric field** is a region around a charged object in which electric force occurs.

- Suppose one charged object is placed in the electric field of a second charged object. The first charged object is either pushed or pulled—repelled or attracted.

- The strength of an electric field depends on how far away the charged object is. The farther away a charged object is, the weaker the electric field is.

*Answer the following questions. Use your textbook and the ideas above.*

**3.** Complete the table about the force around charged objects.

| Force Around a Charged Object | |
|---|---|
| **Term** | **Description** |
| Electric a. _____ | the attraction or repulsion between electric charges |
| Electric b. _____ | a region around a charged object in which electric force occurs |

**4.** The farther away a charged object is, the

_____ the electric field is.

# Static Electricity (page 685)

*Key Concept:* **In static electricity, charges build up on an object, but they do not flow continuously.**

- Most objects usually have no charge. However, objects can become charged.

- If an object loses electrons, it has more protons than electrons. Therefore, it has a positive charge.

- If an object gains electrons, it has more electrons than protons. Therefore, it has a negative charge.

- **Static electricity** is the buildup of charges on an object. *Static* means "not moving." In static electricity, the charges do not flow or move.

*Answer the following questions. Use your textbook and the ideas above.*

**5.** The buildup of charges on an object is called

_____ electricity.

**6.** Is the following sentence true or false? If an object gains electrons, it will have a positive

charge. _____

# Transferring Charge (pages 686–688)

*Key Concept:* **There are three methods by which charges can be transferred to build up static electricity: charging by friction, by conduction, and by induction.**

- An object becomes charged when electrons move from one place to another place.

**Electricity**

- Charging by **friction** is when electrons move from one uncharged object to another object by rubbing. For example, a girl charges by friction when she rubs her socks on the carpet.

- Charging by **conduction** is when electrons move from a charged object to another object by direct contact. You can charge yourself by conduction when you touch a charged object.

- Charging by **induction** is when electrons move to one part of an object due to the electric field of another object. There is no touching in charging by induction.

- You can find out if an object is charged by using an instrument called an electroscope.

*Answer the following questions. Use your textbook and the ideas on page 295 and above.*

**7.** Read each word in the box. In each sentence below, fill in one of the words.

| | | | |
|---|---|---|---|
| induction | friction | conduction | static |

**a.** Charging by_____ is when electrons move from a charged object to another object by direct contact.

**b.** Charging by_____ is when electrons move from one uncharged object to another object by rubbing.

**c.** Charging by_____ is when electrons move to one part of an object due to the electric field of another object.

**Electricity**

8. Which method of transferring charges is shown in the picture below? _____

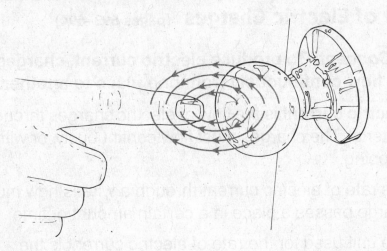

## Static Discharge (pages 688–689)

*Key Concept:* **When a negatively charged object and a positively charged object are brought together, electrons transfer until both objects have the same charge.**

- Charges may build up as static electricity on an object. But the charges do not stay on that object forever.

- The loss of static electricity as charges move from one object to another is called **static discharge**.

- A static discharge often produces a spark. For example, there may be a tiny spark when you touch a metal doorknob. Lightning is another example of static discharge.

*Answer the following questions. Use your textbook and the ideas above.*

9. The loss of static electricity as charges move from one object to another is called _____.

10. Is the following sentence true or false? Thunder is an example of static discharge. _____

# Electric Current (pages 692–699)

## Flow of Electric Charges (pages 693–694)

*Key Concept:* **To produce electric current, charges must flow continuously from one place to another.**

- **Electric current** is the flow of electric charges through a material. The charges must flow continuously, or without stopping.

- The rate of electric current through a wire is how much charge passes a place in a certain amount of time.

- The unit used for the rate of electric current is the ampere. The name can be shortened to *amp* or *A*.

- A current needs a path to follow. An **electric circuit** is an unbroken path through which electric charges flow. An electric circuit is always a complete loop with no breaks in the loop.

- If an electric circuit is complete, charges can flow continuously. If an electric circuit is broken, charges will stop flowing.

*Answer the following questions. Use your textbook and the ideas above.*

1. Read each word in the box. In each sentence below, fill in the correct words.

| electric current | static electricity | electric circuit |
|---|---|---|

   **a.** The continuous flow of electric charges through a material is called _____.

   **b.** An unbroken path through which electric charges flow is a(an) _____.

**2.** Is the following sentence true or false? If an electric circuit is broken, charges will not flow. _____

## Conductors and Insulators (page 695)

*Key Concept:* **A conductor transfers electric charge well. An insulator does not transfer electric charge well.**

- Any material that an electric charge can go through easily is called a **conductor**. Metals are good conductors. Silver, copper, aluminum, and iron are metals.

- Any material that an electric charge has a hard time going through is called an **insulator**. Rubber, glass, plastic, and wood are good insulators.

- The rubber coating on an electric cord is an example of an insulator.

*Answer the following questions. Use your textbook and the ideas above.*

**3.** Complete the table about conductors and insulators.

| Conductors and Insulators | |
|---|---|
| **Term** | **Examples** |
| a. _____ | rubber, glass, plastic, wood |
| b. _____ | silver, copper, aluminum, iron |

**Electricity**

4. Circle the letter of each sentence that is true about conductors and insulators.

   a. Electric charge can flow easily through a conductor.

   b. Electric charge cannot flow easily through an insulator.

   c. Electric charge can flow easily through both conductors and insulators.

## Voltage (pages 696–697)

***Key Concept:* Voltage causes a current in an electric circuit.**

- Charges need energy to flow through a wire. The energy that makes charges flow is called electrical potential energy. A battery, for example, creates an electrical potential energy in an electric circuit.

- **Voltage** is the difference in electrical potential energy between two places in a circuit. Another name for voltage is potential difference. The unit of measure of voltage is the volt, which is abbreviated as V.

- An electric circuit needs a source of energy to have voltage. A **voltage source** creates a potential difference, or voltage, in an electric circuit. A battery is an example of a voltage source. An electric generator is also a voltage source.

*Answer the following questions. Use your textbook and the ideas above.*

5. The difference in electrical potential energy between two places in a circuit is called

   _____.

6. Is the following sentence true or false? The unit of measure of voltage is the amp. _____

**Electricity**

7. The picture below shows an electric circuit. Draw a circle around the voltage source.

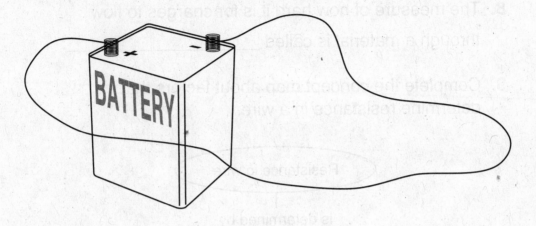

## Resistance (pages 698–699)

***Key Concept:*** **The greater the resistance, the less current there is for a given voltage.**

- **Resistance** is the measure of how hard it is for charges to flow through a material. The unit of measure for resistance is the ohm. The symbol $\Omega$ stands for "ohms."

- How much current there is through a circuit depends on how much resistance there is. The more the resistance there is, the less current there will be.

- How much resistance there is in a wire depends on these four factors:
    1. the material the wire is made of
    2. the length of the wire
    3. the diameter of the wire
    4. the temperature of the wire

- If an electric charge can flow through either of two paths, it will flow through the path with the least resistance.

**Electricity**

Answer the following questions. Use your textbook and the ideas on page 301.

**8.** The measure of how hard it is for charges to flow through a material is called _____.

**9.** Complete the concept map about factors that determine resistance in a wire.

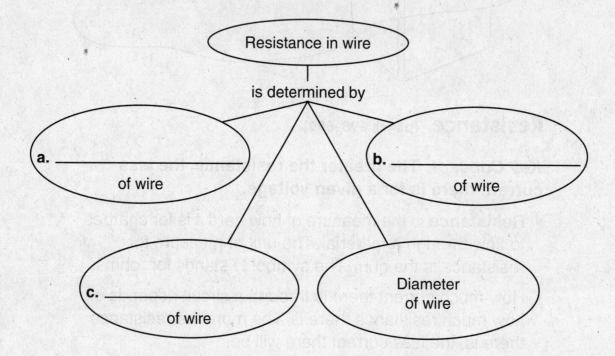

**Electricity**

# Batteries (pages 702–705)

## The First Battery (page 703)

*Key Concept:* **Alessandro Volta built the first electric battery by layering zinc, paper soaked in salt water, and silver.**

- Batteries change chemical energy into electrical energy. **Chemical energy** is energy stored in chemical compounds.

- Alessandro Volta was an Italian scientist who lived around 1800. He built the first battery.

- Volta's first battery contained many layers. Each layer was made of a piece of zinc, a piece of paper soaked in salt water, and a piece of silver. He placed the layers one on top of another.

- Volta used wire to connect the top piece of zinc to the bottom piece of silver. When he connected the wire, his battery produced an electric current.

*Answer the following questions. Use your textbook and the ideas above.*

1. The energy stored in chemical compounds is called
   _____ energy.

2. Alessandro Volta was an Italian scientist who built
   the first _____.

3. Circle the letter of each material that made up part of a layer in Volta's battery.
   a. a piece of zinc
   b. a piece of paper soaked in salt water
   c. a piece of silver

# Electrochemical Cells (pages 704–705)

*Key Concept:* **Chemical reactions occur between the electrolyte and the electrodes in an electrochemical cell. These reactions cause one electrode to become negatively charged and the other electrode to become positively charged.**

- An **electrochemical cell** changes chemical energy into electrical energy. Volta's first battery is an example of an electrochemical cell.

- Two different metals called **electrodes** always make up part of an electrochemical cell. In Volta's cell, the electrodes were silver and zinc.

- An **electrolyte** is a substance that conducts electric current. In Volta's cell, the electrolyte was salt water.

- The part of an electrode that sticks above the surface of the electrolyte is called a **terminal**.

- A **battery** is two or more electrochemical cells. Single electrochemical cells are often called "batteries," too.

- An electrochemical cell in which the electrolyte is a liquid is called a **wet cell**. An electrochemical cell in which the electrolyte is a paste is called a **dry cell**.

*Answer the following questions. Use your textbook and the ideas above.*

4. Circle the letter of each sentence that is true about electrochemical cells.

   a. Single electrochemical cells are often called "batteries."

   b. Chemical reactions occur in electrochemical cells.

   c. In wet cells, the electrolyte is a paste.

5. Draw a line from each term to its meaning.

| Term | Meaning |
|---|---|
| electrochemical cell | **a.** a combination of two or more electrochemical cells |
| electrode | **b.** a substance in an electrochemical cell that conducts electric current |
| electrolyte | **c.** an electrochemical cell in which the electrolyte is a liquid |
| battery | **d.** a device that changes chemical energy into electrical energy |
| wet cell | **e.** a metal in an electrochemical cell |
| dry cell | **f.** an electrochemical cell in which the electrolyte is a paste |

6. The picture shows an electrochemical cell. The arrow points to a part of the cell. Circle the letter of the name of that part.

   **a.** electrode

   **b.** electrolyte

   **c.** terminal

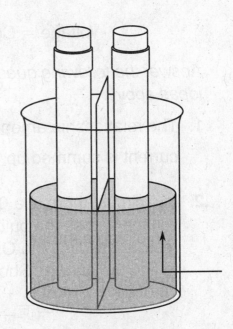

# Electric Circuits and Power

**(pages 706–714)**

## Ohm's Law  (page 707)

***Key Concept:*** Ohm's law says that the resistance is equal to the voltage divided by the current.

- Current, voltage, and resistance are related to one another. The relationship among resistance, voltage, and current is summed up in **Ohm's law**.

- The equation of Ohm's law is:

$$\text{Resistance} = \frac{\text{Voltage}}{\text{Current}}$$

- The units in the equation are:

$$\text{Ohms } (\Omega) = \text{Volts (V)} \div \text{Amps (A)}$$

- You can rearrange Ohm's law to find voltage with this equation:

$$\text{Voltage} = \text{Current} \times \text{Resistance}$$

*Answer the following questions. Use your textbook and the ideas above.*

1. The relationship among resistance, voltage, and current is summed up in_____ law.

2. In a circuit, there is a 0.3-A current in a light bulb. The voltage across the bulb is 12 V. What is the bulb's resistance? Use the Ohm's law equation given above to find the answer. Show your work in the space below.

    Resistance = _____

3. Circle the letter of the equation you could use to find the voltage of a circuit.
   a. Voltage = Current ÷ Resistance
   b. Voltage = Resistance ÷ Current
   c. Voltage = Current × Resistance

## Features of a Circuit (pages 708–709)

*Key Concept:* **First, circuits have devices that are run by electrical energy. Second, a circuit has a source of electrical energy. Third, electric circuits are connected by conducting wires.**

- All circuits have the same three basic features:
  1. All circuits have electrical devices.
  2. All circuits have a source of electrical energy.
  3. All circuits have conducting wires that connect the circuit.

- Radios, appliances, and light bulbs are examples of electrical devices. All these devices resist the flow of electrical energy. As a result, electrical devices are known as resistors.

- Sources of electrical energy in a circuit include batteries, generators, and electric plants. When you plug a radio into a wall socket, the source of electrical energy is your local electric plant.

- Conducting wires complete the path of an electric circuit. Wires allow charges to flow from the energy source to the electric device and back to the energy source.

- Often, a switch is placed in an electric circuit. With a switch, you can turn a device on or off by opening or closing the circuit.

*Answer the following questions. Use your textbook and the ideas on page 307.*

**4.** Circle the letter of each item that is a basic feature of an electric circuit.

   **a.** electrical device

   **b.** source of electric energy

   **c.** conducting wires

**5.** The picture shows a diagram of a circuit. Draw an X beside the resistor.

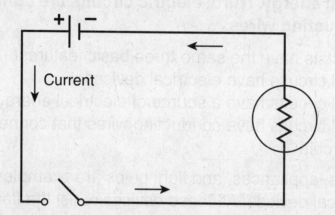

**6.** Is the following sentence true or false? A battery is a source of electric energy. _____

## Series Circuits (page 710)

***Key Concept:* In a series circuit, there is only one path for the current to take.**

- A **series circuit** has all the parts of the circuit connected on one path.

- An example of a series circuit is a circuit with a battery and two light bulbs connected by a single wire.

- Suppose a series circuit has two light bulbs. If one bulb burns out, the other bulb will go out, too. The second bulb goes out because the circuit is broken when the first bulb burns out.

Name _____ Date _____ Class _____

**Electricity**

- If you add resistors to a series circuit, the resistance of the circuit increases.
- An **ammeter** is an instrument used to measure current.

*Answer the following questions. Use your textbook and the ideas on page 308 and above.*

7. Read each word in the box. In each sentence below, fill in the correct word or words.

> ammeter      series circuit      resistor

   a. An electric circuit that has all the parts of the circuit connected on one path is a(an)

   _____.

   b. An instrument used to measure current is a(an)

   _____.

8. Circle the letter of what happens to a light bulb in a series circuit if another light bulb burns out.
   a. The light bulb stays lit.
   b. The light bulb goes out.
   c. The light bulb lights.

9. Is the following sentence true or false? If you add resistors to a series circuit, the resistance of the circuit

   decreases. _____

## Parallel Circuits (pages 711–712)

*Key Concept:* **In a parallel circuit, there are several paths for current to take.**

- A **parallel circuit** has more than one path for current to take. There are separate branches in a parallel circuit. Each resistor may be on its own branch.

- Suppose a parallel circuit has two light bulbs, each on its own branch. If one light bulb burns out, the other light bulb will stay lit. The second bulb stays lit because it is on its own branch.

- If you add branches to a parallel circuit, the overall resistance of the circuit decreases.

- A **voltmeter** measures voltage.

- Electric circuits in your home are parallel circuits.

*Answer the following questions. Use your textbook and the ideas on page 309 and above.*

**10.** Draw a line from each term to its meaning.

| Term | Meaning |
|------|---------|
| parallel circuit | **a.** a device used to measure voltage |
| voltmeter | **b.** an electric circuit that has more than one path for current to take |

**11.** The pictures below show two types of electric circuits. Circle the letter of the parallel circuit.

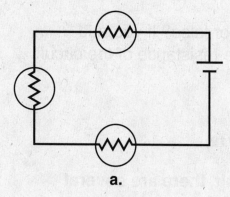

**a.**

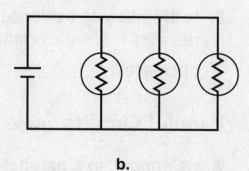

**b.**

**Electricity**

# Electric Power (pages 712–713)

*Key Concept:* **You can calculate power by multiplying voltage by current.**

- All electrical appliances change electrical energy into another form of energy. For example, a hair dryer changes electrical energy into thermal energy.

- **Power** is the rate at which energy is changed from one form to another. The unit of power is the watt, which is abbreviated as W. Each electrical device has a power rating.

- The power of an electrical device depends on the voltage and the current. The equation to calculate power is:

  Power = Voltage × Current

- The units in the power equation are:

  Watts (W) = Volts (V) × Amperes (A)

- You can use the symbols *P* for power, *V* for voltage, and *I* for current. Using these symbols, the power equation can be written this way:

  $$P = VI$$

*Answer the following questions. Use your textbook and the ideas above.*

**12.** The rate at which energy is changed from one form to another is called _____.

**13.** Is the following sentence true or false? The unit of power is the watt. _____

**Electricity**

**14.** A clock radio uses the standard voltage of 120 volts. The clock radio has 0.1 amps of current in it. What is the power rating of the clock radio? Use the equation to calculate power given above. Show your work in the space below.

Power = _____

# Paying for Electrical Energy (page 714)

*Key Concept:* **The total amount of energy used by an appliance is equal to the power of the appliance multiplied by the amount of time the appliance is used.**

- Different appliances change electrical energy into other forms of energy at different rates. The more you use an appliance, the more energy it uses.

- The equation to calculate the amount of energy an appliance uses is:

Energy = Power × Time

- The unit of electrical energy is the kilowatt-hour, which is abbreviated as kWh. One kilowatt is equal to 100 watts.

- The units in the electric-power equation are:

Kilowatt-hours = Kilowatts × Hours

**Electricity**

*Answer the following questions. Use your textbook and the ideas on page 312.*

**15.** Circle the letter of the unit of electrical energy.

    **a.** ampere

    **b.** watt

    **c.** kilowatt-hour

**16.** Is the following sentence true or false? The more you use an appliance, the more energy it uses.

_____

**17.** Circle the letter of the equation used to calculate the amount of energy an appliance uses.

    **a.** Energy = Power $\times$ Time

    **b.** Energy = Power $\div$ Time

    **c.** Power = Energy $\times$ Time

**Electricity**

# Electrical Safety (pages 715–717)

## Personal Safety (pages 715–716)

*Key Concept:* One way to protect people from electric shock and other electrical danger is to provide an alternate path for electric current.

- A **short circuit** is a connection that allows current to take a path of least resistance. For example, a person who touches a downed electric wire may provide a path of least resistance. The electric charge may flow through the person instead of the wire.

- An electric shock can happen when a person receives an electric current from a wire. An electric shock can cause burns and even stop the heart.

- Most buildings have a wire that connects all electric circuits to the ground. A circuit is **grounded** when a wire connects the circuit to the ground. Grounding gives a path for current in case there is a short circuit.

- One way to ground an appliance is to use a third prong. A **third prong** is a little round post on a plug that connects an appliance to a ground wire.

*Answer the following questions. Use your textbook and the ideas above.*

1. Circle the letter of what grounding a circuit does.
   a. Grounding causes a short circuit in a building's electric circuit.
   b. Grounding gives a path for electric current in case there is a short circuit.
   c. Grounding causes burns and can even stop the heart.

**Electricity**

2. Complete the table about electrical safety.

| Electrical Safety | |
| --- | --- |
| **Term** | **Description** |
| a. _____ | a connection that allows current to take a path of least resistance |
| b. _____ | when a wire connects the circuit to the ground |
| c. _____ | a little round post on a plug that connects an appliance to a ground wire |

## Breaking a Circuit (page 717)

*Key Concept:* **In order to prevent circuits from overheating, devices called fuses and circuit breakers are added to circuits.**

• Too much current in a circuit can cause a fire.

• A **fuse** is a device that has a strip of metal that can melt. The metal strip melts when there is too much current. When the metal strip melts, the fuse "blows" and breaks the circuit.

• A **circuit breaker** is a switch that breaks the circuit when current becomes too high.

• When a fuse blows, you have to replace it with a new fuse. When a circuit breaker breaks a circuit, you just have to pull the switch back to reuse the circuit breaker again.

**Electricity**

*Answer the following questions. Use your textbook and the ideas on page 315.*

3. Circle the letter of what too much current in a circuit can cause.

   **a.** grounding

   **b.** fire

   **c.** heart attack

4. Read each word in the box. In each sentence below, fill in the correct word or words.

   | | | |
   |---|---|---|
   | short circuit | circuit breaker | fuse |

   **a.** A switch that breaks the circuit when current becomes too high is a(an) _____.

   **b.** A device that contains a strip of metal that can melt is a(an) _____.

5. Circle the letter of what you can do to reuse a circuit breaker.

   **a.** replace it with a new one

   **b.** throw it away

   **c.** pull the switch back

# What Is Electromagnetism?

(pages 724–728)

## Electric Current and Magnetism (page 725)

*Key Concept:* **An electric current produces a magnetic field.**

- Wherever there is electricity, there is magnetism. **Electromagnetism** is the relationship between electricity and magnetism.

- A compass needle normally points north. When an electric current is present, a compass needle will point in the direction of the current's field. An electric current produces a magnetic field.

- An electric current through a wire produces a magnetic field around the wire. You can use iron filings to show the magnetic field lines around a wire that has a current.

*Answer the following questions. Use your textbook and the ideas above.*

1. The picture below shows iron filings around a wire that has a current. Circle the letter of what the iron filings show.
   a. magnetic field lines
   b. a compass needle
   c. an electric current

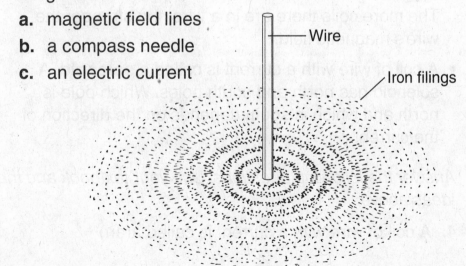

Wire

Iron filings

**Using Electricity and Magnetism**

**2.** The relationship between electricity and magnetism is called _____.

**3.** Circle the letter of what an electric current through a wire produces.

    **a.** parallel circuit

    **b.** compass needle

    **c.** magnetic field

## Solenoids (page 726)

*Key Concept:* **The magnetic field produced by a current has three distinct characteristics. The field can be turned on or off, have its direction reversed, or have its strength changed.**

- You can turn off and on a magnetic field produced by a current in a wire. If you turn the current off, you turn off the magnetic field. If you turn the current on again, you turn on the magnetic field.

- You can change the direction of the magnetic field by changing the direction of the current.

- You can increase a magnetic field produced by a current by twisting a wire into a loop. A loop is also called a coil. The more coils there are in a wire, the stronger the wire's magnetic field.

- A coil of wire with a current is called a **solenoid**. A solenoid has north and south poles. Which pole is north and which is south depends on the direction of the current.

*Answer the following questions. Use your textbook and the ideas above.*

**4.** A coil of wire with a current is called a(an)

_____.

**5.** Circle the letter of each sentence that is true about a magnetic field produced by a current.

    **a.** The strength of the field always remains the same.

    **b.** The field can be turned on or off.

    **c.** The field can have its direction changed.

**6.** Is the following sentence true or false? The more coils there are in a wire, the stronger the wire's

magnetic field. _____

# Electromagnets (pages 727–728)

*Key Concept:* **An electromagnet is a strong magnet that can be turned on and off.**

- You can put a ferromagnetic material inside the coils of a solenoid. For example, iron is a ferromagnetic material. When you put iron inside a solenoid, the strength of the magnetic field increases.

- A solenoid with a ferromagnetic material inside is called an **electromagnet**. You can turn an electromagnet on and off by turning the current on and off.

- You can increase the strength of an electromagnet by increasing the current in the solenoid.

- You can increase the strength of an electromagnet by adding more loops of wire to the solenoid.

- You can increase the strength of an electromagnet by using a stronger ferromagnetic material inside the solenoid.

- Electromagnets have many uses. They are used in computers and doorbells. Electromagnets are also used to lift heavy objects.

**Using Electricity and Magnetism**

*Answer the following questions. Use your textbook and the ideas on page 319.*

7. A solenoid with a ferromagnetic material inside is called a(an) _____.

8. Circle the letter of each way you could increase the strength of an electromagnet.
    a. You could use a stronger ferromagnetic material inside the solenoid.
    b. You could increase the current in the solenoid.
    c. You could add more loops of wire to the solenoid.

9. The picture below shows two electromagnets. Circle the letter of the electromagnet that is the stronger one.

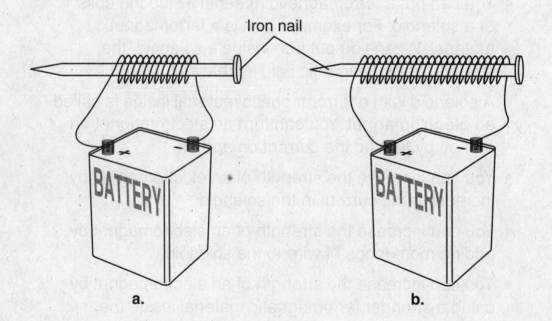

Iron nail

a.　　　　　　　　　　　　　　b.

# Electricity, Magnetism, and Motion (pages 729–733)

## Electrical Energy and Motion (page 730)

*Key Concept:* When a wire with a current is placed in a magnetic field, electrical energy is transformed into mechanical energy.

- A magnet can move a wire with a current. The magnetic field of the magnet interacts with the magnetic field of the wire with a current. The result is that the wire moves.

- The ability to move an object is called **energy**. The energy of electric currents is called **electrical energy**.

- The energy of motion is called **mechanical energy**.

- Electrical energy changes into mechanical energy when a wire with a current is placed in a magnetic field. The electrical energy produces the magnetic field in the wire with a current. The movement that results is mechanical energy.

*Answer the following questions. Use your textbook and the ideas above.*

1. Circle the letter of what happens when a wire with a current is placed in a magnetic field.
   a. The wire moves.
   b. The circuit breaks.
   c. The magnetic field turns off.

2. Is the following sentence true or false? Mechanical energy changes into electrical energy when a wire with a current is placed in a magnetic field. _____

**Using Electricity and Magnetism**

**3.** Draw a line from each term to its meaning.

| Term | Meaning |
|------|---------|
| energy | **a.** the energy of motion |
| | **b.** the ability to move an object |
| electrical energy | **c.** the energy of electric currents |
| mechanical energy | |

## Galvanometers (page 731)

*Key Concept:* **An electric current is used to turn the pointer of a galvanometer.**

- A **galvanometer** is a device that measures small currents.

- A galvanometer contains an electromagnet. The electromagnet is between the opposite poles of two permanent magnets.

- A current in the electromagnet produces a magnetic field. The electromagnet's magnetic field interacts with the magnetic fields of the permanent magnets. This interaction causes the electromagnet to move.

- A pointer is attached to the electromagnet in a galvanometer. When the electromagnet moves, the pointer moves. A scale shows how much the pointer moves. The current through the electromagnet is measured on the scale.

*Answer the following questions. Use your textbook and the ideas above.*

**4.** A device that measures small currents is a(an)

_____.

5.  Circle the letter of each sentence that is true about a galvanometer.

    a.  A galvanometer contains an electromagnet.

    b.  The electromagnet never moves inside a galvanometer.

    c.  The electromagnet's magnetic field interacts with the magnetic fields of the permanent magnets.

## Electric Motors (pages 732–733)

*Key Concept:* **An electric motor transforms electrical energy into mechanical energy.**

*   An **electric motor** uses an electric current to turn an axle. An axle is a rod. For example, an electric motor turns the axle of a fan. The fan blades are connected to the turning axle.

*   An electric motor works by changing electrical energy into mechanical energy.

*   In an electric motor, a loop of wire spins continuously. It spins continuously by changing the direction of the current at each half turn of the loop. Every half turn of the axle, the current reverses. First it goes one way, and then it goes the opposite way.

*   The part of an electric motor that reverses the current is called a commutator. A commutator is a ring split in half.

*Answer the following questions. Use your textbook and the ideas above.*

6.  A device that uses an electric current to turn an axle

    is a(an) _____.

**Using Electricity and Magnetism**

7. Circle the letter of the sentence that explains how an electric motor works.

   a. An electric motor works by changing mechanical energy into electrical energy.

   b. An electric motor works by changing mechanical energy into a magnetic field.

   c. An electric motor works by changing electrical energy into mechanical energy.

8. The picture below shows the parts of an electric motor. Circle the part that reverses the current with each half turn.

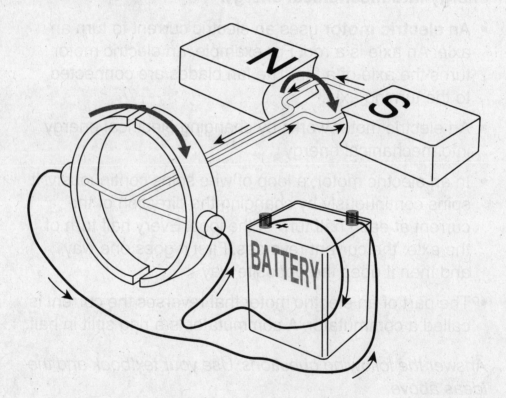

# Electricity From Magnetism
(pages 736–743)

## Induction of Electric Current (pages 736–739)

*Key Concept:* **An electric current is induced in a conductor when the conductor moves through a magnetic field.**

- Motion can produce electrical energy. Suppose you move a conductor, such as a wire, through a magnetic field. By doing this, you will create an electrical current in the conductor.

- **Electromagnetic induction** is when an electric current is created in a conductor by moving the conductor through a magnetic field. This is called "inducing a current." Current that is made by moving a conductor through a magnetic field is called induced current.

- You can induce a current in two ways:
  1. You can move the conductor through the magnetic field.
  2. You can move a magnet through a coil of wire.

- An induced current may flow in only one direction. A current that flows in only one direction is called **direct current**. Direct current is also called DC.

- An induced current may reverse directions very quickly over and over again. A current that reverses direction repeatedly is called **alternating current**. Alternating current is also called AC.

*Answer the following questions. Use your textbook and the ideas above.*

1. Electromagnetic induction is the process of creating an electric current in a conductor by moving the conductor through a(n) _____.

**Using Electricity and Magnetism**

2. Circle the letter of what the current is called that is made by moving a conductor through a magnetic field.

    **a.** reversed current

    **b.** induced current

    **c.** magnetic current

3. Complete the table about kinds of induced current.

| Kinds of Induced Current | |
| --- | --- |
| **Kind of Induced Current** | **Description** |
| **a.** _____ current | a current that flows in only one direction |
| **b.** _____ current | a current that reverses direction repeatedly |

## Generators (pages 740–741)

*Key Concept:* **A generator uses motion in a magnetic field to produce an electric current.**

• An **electric generator** changes mechanical energy into electrical energy.

• An electric generator is the opposite of an electric motor. Remember, an electric motor changes electrical energy into mechanical energy.

• Some generators produce alternating current. They are called AC generators.

• Some generators produce direct current. They are called DC generators.

• The electric company uses giant generators to produce electrical energy for your home and school.

**Using Electricity and Magnetism**

*Answer the following questions. Use your textbook and the ideas on page 326.*

**4.** Circle the letter of a device that changes mechanical energy into electrical energy.

   **a.** electric generator

   **b.** electric motor

   **c.** galvanometer

**5.** Is the following sentence true or false? An electric generator is the opposite of an electric motor. _____

**6.** Draw a line from each term to its description.

| Term | Description |
| --- | --- |
| AC generator | **a.** a generator that produces direct current |
| DC generator | **b.** a generator that produces alternating current |

## Transformers (pages 741–743)

*Key Concept: A transformer is a device that increases or decreases voltage.*

- Electric companies send electrical energy through wires at high voltages. Your home, though, uses electrical energy at low voltages. Transformers are used to change the voltage of an electric current.

- A **transformer** is made up of two coils of wire, each wrapped around an iron core.

- One coil of a transformer—called the primary coil—is connected to an alternating current. The other coil—called the secondary coil—is not connected to a source of electricity.

**Using Electricity and Magnetism**

- Alternating current flows through the primary coil of a transformer. This causes a magnetic field to change as the current alternates. The changing magnetic field induces a current in the secondary coil.

- A transformer can either increase voltage or decrease voltage. A **step-up transformer** increases voltage. In a step-up transformer, there are more loops in the secondary coil than in the primary coil.

- A **step-down transformer** decreases voltage. In a step-down transformer, there are fewer loops in the secondary coil than in the primary coil.

- Transformers allow safe transfer of electrical energy from generating plants to homes and other buildings.

*Answer the following questions. Use your textbook and the ideas on page 327 and above.*

**7.** A device that is used to change the voltage of an

electric current is a(an) _____.

**8.** Circle the letter of each sentence that is true about a transformer.
   **a.** The primary coil is connected to an alternating current.
   **b.** The primary coil is not connected to a source of electricity.
   **c.** The secondary coil is not connected to a source of electricity.

**9.** Circle the letter of what goes through the primary coil of a transformer that causes a magnetic field to change.
   **a.** alternating current
   **b.** magnetic current
   **c.** direct current

**Using Electricity and Magnetism**

**10.** Is the following sentence true or false? Step-up
transformers are used to step down voltage before
the current is used in a home. _____

**11.** The pictures below show two types of transformers.
Circle the letter of the picture of a step-up transformer.

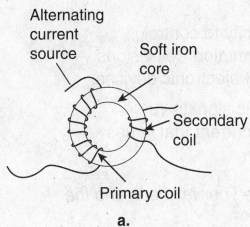

a.

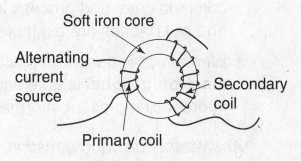

b.

**Electronics**

# Electronic Signals and Semiconductors (pages 750–754)

## Introduction (page 750)

*Key Concept:* **Electronics is based on electronic signals.**

- **Electronics** is the use of electricity to control, communicate, and process information. Televisions and cell phones are examples of electronic devices.

- Electronics is based on electronic signals. An **electronic signal** is an electric current that varies in order to represent information.

*Answer the following question. Use your textbook and the ideas above.*

1. Draw a line from each term to its meaning.

| Term | Meaning |
|------|---------|
| electronics | **a.** an electric current that varies in order to represent information |
| electronic signal | **b.** the use of electricity to control, communicate, and process information |

## Analog and Digital Signals (page 751)

*Key Concept:* **There are two basic kinds of electronic signals: analog signals and digital signals.**

- The two basic kinds of electronic signals represent information in different ways.

- An **analog signal** is an electric current that is varied smoothly to represent information.

- Think of a thermometer with liquid in a tube. As the temperature rises and falls, the liquid goes up and down smoothly. An analog signal also varies smoothly.

- A **digital signal** is an electric current that uses pulses to represent information. The signal does not vary smoothly but varies in steps.

- Think of a digital thermometer. As the temperature rises, the numbers on a digital thermometer change suddenly by whole degrees. A digital signal also varies in steps.

*Answer the following questions. Use your textbook and the ideas on page 330 and above.*

2. Complete the table about kinds of electronic signals.

| Kinds of Electronic Signals | |
|---|---|
| **Kind of Electronic Signal** | **Description** |
| a._____ signal | an electric current that is varied smoothly to represent information |
| b._____ signal | an electric current that uses pulses to represent information |

3. Is the following sentence true or false? An analog signal represents information like a thermometer that has liquid in a tube. _____

**Electronics**

# Semiconductor Devices (pages 752–754)

*Key Concept:* **The two types of semiconductors can be combined in different ways to make diodes, transistors, and integrated circuits.**

- Electronic devices use semiconductors to vary current. A **semiconductor** is a material that conducts current better than an insulator but not as well as a conductor.

- There are two types of semiconductors:
  1. An n-type semiconductor can give off electrons.
  2. A p-type semiconductor can receive an electron.

- Scientists combine n-type and p-type semiconductors in layers. Layers of semiconductors are used to control current in electronic devices.

- A **diode** is an electronic part that has a n-type semiconductor and a p-type semiconductor joined together. Diodes can be used to change alternating current to direct current.

- A **transistor** is an electronic part that has one type of semiconductor between two layers of the other type of semiconductor. A transistor can be used to increase an electronic signal.

- An **integrated circuit** is a thin slice of semiconductor that contains many diodes, transistors, and other electronic parts. Integrated circuits are also called chips.

*Answer the following questions. Use your textbook and the ideas above.*

4. Circle the letter of a material that conducts current better than an insulator but not as well as a conductor.
   a. electric wire
   b. semiconductor
   c. integrate circuit

**5.** Read each word in the box. In each sentence below, fill in the correct word or words.

| | | | |
|---|---|---|---|
| diode | integrated circuit | transistor | fuse |

   **a.** A thin slice of semiconductor that contains many diodes, transistors, and other electronic parts is a(an) _____.

   **b.** An electronic part that has a n-type semiconductor and a p-type semiconductor joined together is a(an) _____.

   **c.** An electronic part that has one type of semiconductor between two layers of the other type of semiconductor is a(an) _____.

**6.** The pictures below show a diode and a transistor. Circle the letter of the picture of a diode.

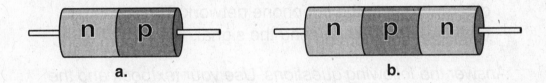

         **a.**                               **b.**

# Electronic Communication

**(pages 756–762)**

## Telephones (pages 756–757)

*Key Concept:* In a telephone, sound is transformed into an electronic signal that is transmitted and then transformed back into sound.

- A telephone has three main parts: a transmitter, a receiver, and a dialing mechanism.

- A **transmitter** changes sound into an electronic signal. A transmitter in a telephone is where you speak.

- The electronic signal from the transmitter travels through wires to a receiver in another telephone. The receiver of a telephone is in the earpiece. A **receiver** changes an electronic signal back into sounds.

- The dialing mechanism of a telephone is usually the pad of numbers that you can push. Each button sends a different tone to the telephone network. The tones tell the network where to send the signal.

*Answer the following questions. Use your textbook and the ideas above.*

1. Circle the letter of each item that is a main part of a telephone.
   - **a.** transmitter
   - **b.** receiver
   - **c.** dialing mechanism

2. In a telephone transmitter, sound is changed into an electronic _____.

3. Circle the letter of a telephone's dialing mechanism.

   a. the part of the telephone that you talk into

   b. the number pad on the telephone

   c. the part of the telephone where you hear sound

## Sound Recordings (pages 758–759)

***Key Concept:* Sound can be reproduced using an analog device such as a phonograph or a digital device such as a CD player.**

- Sound recordings communicate information using electronic signals.

- A phonograph, or record player, is an analog device. A phonograph plays plastic records. When a phonograph plays a record, a needle runs along a groove in the record. The wavy pattern in the groove is changed into an analog signal. A speaker changes the analog signal back into sound.

- A CD player is a digital device. A CD contains tiny holes called pits and level areas called flats. A beam of light reads these pits and flats and changes the pattern into a digital signal. A speaker changes the digital signal back into sound.

*Answer the following questions. Use your textbook and the ideas above.*

4. Circle the letter of a digital device used to reproduce sound.

   a. CD player

   b. phonograph

   c. plastic record

**5.** Is the following sentence true or false? Sound recordings communicate information using electronic signals. _____

## Radio (pages 760–761)

*Key Concept:* **Voices or music on an AM or FM radio station are electronic signals carried by an electromagnetic wave.**

- The process of radio transmission begins at a radio station. There, sounds are changed into an electronic signal called an audio signal.

- A transmitter at the radio station combines the audio signal with an electromagnetic wave. The electromagnetic wave that carries the audio signal is sent out through an antenna in all directions.

- There are two ways to change a wave to carry an electronic signal. One way is to change the amplitude of the wave. Changing the amplitude of a wave to carry an electronic signal is called amplitude modulation (AM).

- The other way is to change the frequency of the wave. Changing the frequency of a wave to carry an electronic signal is called frequency modulation (FM).

- Your radio receives that electromagnetic wave and separates the audio signal from it. The radio's speaker changes the audio signal back into sound.

*Answer the following questions. Use your textbook and the ideas above.*

**6.** Circle the letter of what a radio station transmitter combines an audio signal with.

   **a.** a compact disc

   **b.** a dialing mechanism

   **c.** electromagnetic wave

**Electronics**

7. Circle the letter of the place where an audio signal is separated from the electromagnetic wave that carries it.

   a. radio station

   b. phonograph

   c. radio speaker

8. The pictures show two ways that a wave can be modulated. Circle the letter of the picture that shows amplitude modulation.

   a.

   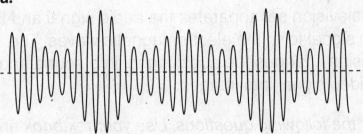

   b.

   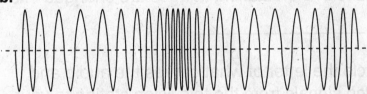

**Electronics**

# Television (pages 761-762)

***Key Concept:*** **Electromagnetic waves can be used to carry images as well as sound.**

- The process of television transmission begins at a television station. There, sounds are changed into an electronic signal called an audio signal. Images are changed into video signals.

- The audio and video signals are combined with electromagnetic waves. The electromagnetic waves carry the audio and video signals to your television set.

- The television set separates the audio signal and the video signal form the electromagnetic waves. The television changes the audio signal into sound and the video signal into images.

*Answer the following questions. Use your textbook and the ideas above.*

9. At a television station, images are changed into

   _____ signals.

10. Circle the letter of what carries the audio and video signals from the television station to your television set.
    a. transistors
    b. semiconductors
    c. electromagnetic waves

**Electronics**

# Computers (pages 763–769)

## What Is a Computer? (pages 763–764)

*Key Concept:* **Computer information is represented in the binary system.**

- A **computer** is an electronic device that stores, changes, and finds information.

- A computer stores information in the binary system. The **binary system** is a number system that uses only two digits—0 and 1.

- You use a number system every day that uses the base 10. The base number of the binary system is 2.

- Computers use the binary system because electronic signals can represent 0 and 1. A switch in the off position represents 0. A switch in the on position represents 1.

- Each 1 or 0 in the binary system is called a bit. Eight bits are called a byte.

*Answer the following questions. Use your textbook and the ideas above.*

1. An electronic device that stores, changes, and finds information is called a(an) _____.

2. Circle the letter of each digit that a binary system uses to represent numbers.
   a. 0
   b. 1
   c. 2

3. Is the following sentence true or false? Eight bits is called a kilobyte. _____

Electronics

## Computer Hardware (pages 765–766)

***Key Concept:*** **Computer hardware includes a central processing unit, input devices, output devices, and memory storage devices.**

- The physical parts of a computer make up the computer's **hardware**. For example, the computer screen—called the monitor—is part of the computer's hardware.

- The **central processing unit** directs everything the computer does. It is also called the CPU. Sometimes, people think of the CPU simply as the computer.

- An **input device** is hardware that feeds data into the CPU. Input devices include a keyboard, mouse, joystick, and scanner.

- An **output device** is hardware that puts out data from the CPU. The main output device is the monitor, which sometimes people call the screen. Printers and speakers are other output devices.

- Computers store information in their memory. There are two main types of computer memory:
  1. Memory within the CPU is called internal memory.
  2. Devices outside the CPU are called external memory. Disks are examples of external memory.

*Answer the following questions. Use your textbook and the ideas above.*

4. Circle the letter of each item that is part of a computer's hardware.
   a. monitor
   b. keyboard
   c. mouse

**Electronics**

5. Complete the table about computer hardware.

| Computer Hardware | |
| --- | --- |
| **Permanent Parts** | **Examples or Description** |
| a. _____ _____ | the brain of the computer |
| b. _____ | keyboard, mouse, or joystick |
| c. _____ | monitor, printer or speaker |
| d. _____ _____ | chip within the CPU |
| e. _____ _____ | disks |

6. The picture shows the hardware of a computer. Draw an X on the CPU.

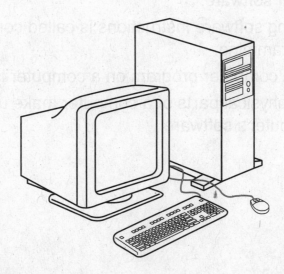

Name _____ Date _____ Class _____

**Electronics**

## Computer Software (pages 767–768)

*Key Concept:* **Software is a set of instructions that directs the computer hardware to perform operations on stored information.**

- **Software** tells a computer what to do. Each computer program on a computer is software.

- There are two kinds of software. One kind is called the operating system of the computer. An operating system is the set of basic instructions that keep a computer running. One common operating system is called DOS. Windows® is a type of operating system that runs many computers.

- Another kind of software is called applications software. Applications are the programs on your computer. Each game or word processing program is an application.

- Writing software instructions is called computer programming. **Computer programmers** use special computer languages to write the instructions for computers.

*Answer the following questions. Use your textbook and the ideas above.*

**7.** Circle the letter of each sentence that is true about computer software.

　**a.** Writing software instructions is called computer programming.

　**b.** Each computer program on a computer is software.

　**c.** The physical parts of a computer make up the computer's software.

**Electronics**

8. Computer _____ use special computer languages to write the instructions for computers.

9. Complete the concept map about kinds of computer software.

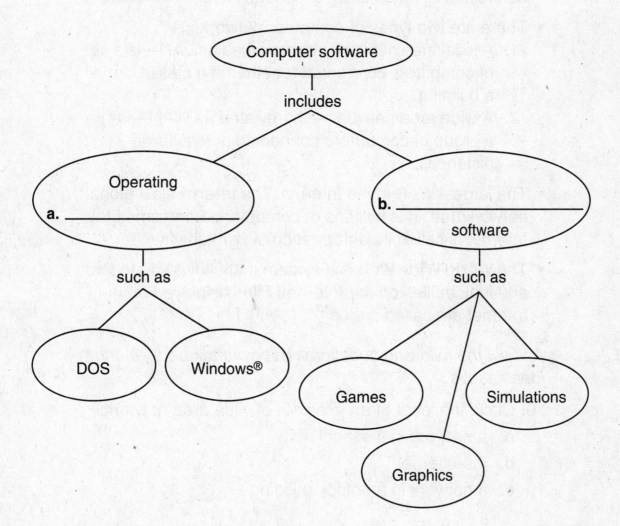

## Computer Networks (pages 768–769)

***Key Concept:*** **A computer network allows people in different locations to share information and software.**

- A **computer network** is a group of computers connected by wires or by telephone lines.

- There are two types of computer networks:
  1. A local area network—abbreviated as LAN—is a set of computers connected together in a classroom or a building.
  2. A wide area network—abbreviated as WAN—is a group of computers connected across large distances.

- The largest WAN in the Internet. The **Internet** is a global network that links millions of computers. Sometimes the Internet is called the information superhighway.

- The **World Wide Web** is a system that allows you to find and look at files on the Internet. Files displayed on the Internet are called pages.

*Answer the following questions. Use your textbook and the ideas above.*

**10.** Circle the letter of an example of wide area network.

    **a.** a network in a school

    **b.** the Internet

    **c.** a network in an office building

**Electronics**

**11.** Draw a line from each term to its meaning.

| **Term** | **Meaning** |
|---|---|
| computer network | **a.** a system that allows you to find and look at files on the Internet |
| Internet | **b.** a group of computers connected by wires or by telephone lines |
| World Wide Web | **c.** a global network that links millions of computers |